Home Canning

By the Editors of Sunset Books and
Sunset Magazine

Lane Publishing Co. • Menlo Park, California

Foreword

Preserving food—once thought of as grandma's specialty—has recently come to enjoy a surge of popularity with people of all ages. Primary reasons for this are the savings made possible and the personal satisfaction of "putting up" foods.

The booming activity of home gardening has also contributed to the revival of interest in home preserving. As food prices soar, many home flower beds have been converted into productive vegetable gardens. Some prolific crops—tomatoes and cucumbers, for instance—can produce much more in one growing season than a single family can consume. Canning, freezing, or drying such surpluses can cut down on needless wastage of your hard-won crops. Additionally, whether you have a garden or not, putting up food allows you to take maximum advantage of good seasonal buys at your local produce stands.

The supplies needed for preserving foods are modest in cost; canning requires jars, lids, ring bands, and a few shelves in the pantry or garage for storage; freezing requires some plastic containers and a freezer; drying uses only a few jars or plastic bags and minimal storage space.

Those who never have tried their hand at putting up food will find this book to be a valuable step-by-step primer. Those with some experience will find new and imaginative recipes to try. Beginners and experts alike will find this to be—above all—an easy-to-use reference book.

We wish to acknowledge with thanks the special checking and consultation of Dr. Robert Cain, Department of Food Science and Technology, Oregon State University, Corvallis, Oregon; Mary Lou Williamson of Ball Corporation, Muncie, Indiana; Cozetta Farley of Kerr Glass Manufacturing Corporation, Sand Springs, Oklahoma; and the Division of Agricultural Science, University of California at Berkeley.

Edited by Judith A. Gaulke

Special Consultant: Dr. George K. York
Food Technologist
University of California at Davis

Staff Consultants: Annabel Post
Home Economics Editor, Sunset Magazine
Kandace Esplund
Staff Home Economist, Sunset Magazine

Illustrations: Nancy Lawton

Design: JoAnn/Masaoka

Cover: Photograph by Norman A. Plate

Photography: Glenn M. Christiansen, 6, 60, 82; Darrow M. Watt, 4.

Editor, Sunset Books: David E. Clark

Contents

Special Features

Canning

Sometimes all it takes is a prolific apricot tree in the backyard or a good buy on tomatoes at a roadside stand to get you interested in home canning. Or you may be lucky enough to have an entire garden full of fresh vegetables at home, and you'd really like to know how to enjoy them all year round. More and more people are discovering (and rediscovering) canning as a fun thing to do as well as a good way to save money.

If you are a newcomer to canning, rest assured that with the right equipment and fresh, wholesome produce, anyone who follows the recommended canning procedures can end up with colorful jars of delicious, safe foods. After you get into it, you'll be amazed at how much can be put up in a short space of time, especially when two or three friends get together and make a day of it.

All sorts of questions arise when you first consider canning—what foods to can, what process to use, what safety precautions to follow.

This book answers all these questions, and more.

So...what happens in canning?

There's no special magic to it. When fruits or vegetables are packed into a canning jar, fitted with a special, self-sealing lid, and then heated sufficiently, this is what happens: high heat kills any dangerous organisms that could cause food spoilage in the jar; it also causes contents of the jar to expand, driving out any air left inside. When the jar cools, the vacuum created inside pulls the lid down to the jar mouth for a tight seal. Unless that seal is broken (or unless the food wasn't handled properly in the canning process or wasn't fit for canning), no organisms that cause spoilage can enter (see *Methods of canning* on page 7).

Use the right equipment

It's very important to use the right equipment to avoid any possibility of food spoilage. Everything from the canning jars to the right canning kettle must be considered. To save money, you might want to share equipment expenses with a friend; then you can take turns canning or do it together.

Canning jars, made of tempered glass that can withstand high temperatures, are a must; you can recognize them by the manufacturer's name or fancy pattern blown into the glass. Sold in houseware departments and grocery stores, they come in ½-pint, pint, 1½-pint, and quart sizes. The wide-mouth jars are most convenient for packing larger pieces of fruit; small jars are good for jams and jelly. Special fancy jars and lids are available just for jelly.

The jars you buy prepared food in, such as quart mayonnaise jars, should never be used for home canning because they won't seal properly and they may break during canning under the intense heat.

Old-fashioned canning jars—called *lightning jars*—with glass lids that clamp down over rubber rings can be used if they are made of tempered glass (those sold in gift shops usually are not).

Left to right: **1.** *Food chopper;* **2.** *water bath canning kettle with lid and wire basket;* **3.** *steam pressure canner;* **4.** *wide-mouth canning funnel;* **5.** *canning jars, lids and ring bands;* **6.** *mercury-type thermometer;* **7.** *food mill;* **8.** *jar lifter;* **9.** *colander;* **10.** *automatic timer;* **11.** *wire strainer.*

To use, fit wet rubber ring to the little sealing ledge on the neck of the filled jar. Put on the glass lid so it rests on rubber ring. Grasp the longest of the two wire clamps (bails), pulling it up to a little groove in the glass lid. Leave the little wire up while the food inside is being canned; then immediately clamp the little wire down to seal the jar as you take it out of the canner. One drawback—it is hard to tell if these jars have sealed once processed.

Canning lids and ring bands are included when you buy new canning jars. The ring bands can be used over and over if in good condition, *but the lids must be replaced each time* because the sealing composition is no longer effective once it has been used.

Zinc caps with porcelain linings and rubber rings were once popular, but today they are very hard to find. If you were lucky enough to inherit some from Grandma, they can still be used if they are in good condition. To use, fit a wet rubber ring down on the shoulder of an empty jar—don't stretch the ring unnecessarily. Pack the jar, wipe the ring and jar rim clean, screw the cap down firmly, and turn it back ¼ inch before canning. As soon as you take the jar from the canner, screw the cap down tightly to complete the seal.

A canning kettle and lid are necessary for canning fruits, fruit juices, fruit purées, tomatoes, and most pickles. It has to be deep enough so that the tops of the jars of food are covered by at least 1 inch of boiling water. Be aware that many smaller canners on the market are not deep enough to hold quart jars. You can improvise with a large stock pot and cover, using a cake rack in the bottom to rest jars on.

A steam pressure canner is the only home-canning device that can apply enough heat long enough to insure the safe canning of vegetables, meat, poultry, and fish, which are especially susceptible to spoilage if not canned properly. The steam pressure canner is a heavy kettle with a cover that locks down to become steamtight. The cover is fitted with a safety valve, a petcock vent, and a pressure gauge. There are two types of canners available; one has a weighted gauge and the other has a dial. A weighted gauge automatically limits pressure by a control preset for 5, 10, or 15 pounds. The dial control indicates pressure on a numbered instrument. (All our home canning is done at 10 pounds pressure.) The canner must be in good working order, and the pressure gauge dial should be checked for accuracy each season before using, either with the manufacturer or with your county cooperative extension service. (You can also use it as a regular canning kettle for canning fruits by leaving the lid ajar and the vents wide open; but a regular canning kettle can never be used in place of a steam pressure canner.) Follow manufacturer's directions for using your particular steam pressure canner.

The small, everyday "pressure cooker" saucepan designed for fast cooking is not suitable for canning.

Helpful canning accessories include a colander or wire basket for scalding (blanching) fruits and vegetables to loosen their skins for peeling before canning, a food mill, a food chopper for grinding up foods, a wire strainer, a wide-mouth canning funnel for easy filling of jars, a jar lifter for handling hot jars, an accurate mercury-type thermometer to check temperatures, and an automatic timer to help you remember length of cooking time. (See adjacent photograph of canning equipment.)

Methods of canning

Safe canning is what it's all about. Step-by-step canning directions for fruits, vegetables, and meats will be handled individually throughout this chapter. But basically, there are two methods of canning—the *boiling water method* and the *steam pressure method*.

The boiling water method can be safely used for all fruits, fruit juices, and fruit purées, as well as for tomatoes and cucumber pickles (but not all pickled vegetables—it depends on the proportion of vinegar). These are fruits and vegetables that, because of their high acidity, discourage bacteria growth.

Use the canning kettle described on page 6, boiling water provides enough heat around the jars of food in the canner to destroy the organisms that might cause spoilage in fruits, tomatoes, pickles, and relishes.

The steam pressure method must be used when canning all other vegetables (the "low-acid" vegetables), meats, poultry, and fish. They should be processed in jars at 10 pounds pressure at sea level in the special steam pressure canner described at left.

What about those canning dangers?

Nearly everyone has heard about a deadly poisoning called *botulism*. The organisms that cause it have some peculiar characteristics. They live without air inside a sealed jar, are not destroyed at the temperature of boiling water (212° F), and are not easily detected when a jar is opened. But they cannot survive in the acid environment provided naturally by fresh, fully ripened fruits, pickles, and high-acid tomato varieties (check with your local county extension service for best varieties for canning)—unless the tomatoes are past maturity and have lost their natural acidity.

Still, the botulism bacteria can thrive in jars of other vegetables, meats, poultry, or fish; that is why these foods must *always* be canned in the steam pressure canner to supply enough sustained heat (240° F) to kill any harmful bacteria. For more information on botulism, see pages 45–46.

Other types of food spoilage that might occur if jars of fruit are not sealed properly are easily detected. If the food smells bad or is soft, discolored, or moldy, discard it without tasting. When in doubt, throw it out!

Canning Fresh Fruits

When it comes to fresh fruits and tomatoes, can them confidently, using the boiling water method described on page 7. You just fill hot canning jars with food and put them into a canning kettle full of simmering water; then heat the food for the specified length of time. You can use either a kettle made especially for canning or any kettle large enough that the jars, when placed on a rack in the kettle bottom, will have at least 1 inch of water over their tops.

Getting the fruit into the jars

There are two ways of packing fruit into jars. The simplest way, sometimes called "*raw pack,*" is to put raw fruit right into the jars and then pour hot syrup over it. (This method is good for most small or soft fruits, such as apricots.)

The second method, sometimes called "*hot pack,*" is to cook the fruit briefly in syrup, pack hot fruit into the jars, and then pour the hot syrup over the fruit. (This method is best for large fruit pieces, such as peach and pear halves—they shrink some in cooking and become more flexible, so you can usually get more into the jar, and they are less likely to float up in the syrup after processing.)

Protecting fruit colors

Some fruits have a tendency to darken after they are cut; the canning charts, pages 12–13, indicate which ones need to be treated. An effective way to prevent darkening is to cut the fruit directly into a solution of 2 tablespoons each of salt and vinegar and 1 gallon of water. Do not leave the fruit in the solution longer than 20 minutes, and rinse the fruit before putting it into jars. Or use a commercial antidarkening agent or ascorbic acid, following the package directions (usually about 3 tablespoons powder to 2 quarts of water).

Is sugar necessary?

You could can without sugar, but some sweetening improves the flavor and appearance of most fruit; it also keeps fruits firmer and helps prevent them from floating in the jars. You have to pour a liquid of some kind over the fruit when the jars are packed; it can be a syrup made of water and sugar or honey (or some of each), a fruit juice (with or without sweetening), or just water. You can make juice by crushing soft fruit, heating it, and then straining it.

The following table gives recommended proportions of sweetener to water and the syrup yield of each. All the syrups have good flavor and texture, but those with the highest proportions of sugar will usually make the most attractive product.

If you want to use honey, choose a mild-flavored one, such as clover. A higher proportion of honey than suggested masks the flavor of the fruit. For the same reason, brown sugar, raw sugar, molasses, and sorghum should not be used. You'll need 1 to 1½ cups syrup for each quart of fruit. Combine the sugar or honey with water in a saucepan and heat to boiling until dissolved.

PROPORTIONS (Cups)	YIELD (Cups)
Light syrup	
2 sugar, 4 water	5
1 honey, 1 sugar, 4 water	5½
1 honey, 3 water	4
Medium syrup	
3 sugar, 4 water	5½
1 honey, 2 sugar, 4 water	6
2 honey, 2 water	4
Heavy syrup	
4 3/4 sugar, 4 water	6½

Step-by-step canning for fruits and tomatoes

1) Have ready a regular canning kettle (see page 6), jars, lids, ring bands, and other helpful accessories (see page 7). Thoroughly wash canning jars and bands and discard jars with nicks or sharp edges on the rim that might prevent a good seal. Discard rusted or bent ring bands, for they will not tighten onto the jars properly. Because jars must also be hot when you fill them, a dishwasher is ideal both for washing jars and for keeping them hot. Scald jar lids in boiling water; keep in very hot water until time to use. (If you don't have a dishwasher you can just keep the jars filled with hot water.)

Check jar rims for nicks or cracks

2) Pick a variety of fruit or tomato known to be a good canner. For recommended varieties and specific directions for preparing individual fruits, see the chart on pages 12 and 13. It also indicates which fruits need to be treated to prevent darkening after they are cut (see information on page 8, *Protecting fruit colors*). Fruits and tomatoes should be ripened to full flavor (but not overripe) and free of blemishes.

Prepare fruit for canning

3) Place the rack in the canning kettle and fill the kettle about half full with hot water. Place the kettle, covered, on the range to heat. In a large teakettle or other pan, heat additional water to add later.

4) Make the syrup of your choice for fruit (see page 8). Heat the syrup until the sugar or honey is dissolved; keep it hot (don't let it boil down). Omit steps 4-5 for tomatoes (see chart on page 13).

5) Fill clean, hot jars one at a time; if necessary, you can reheat a jar by immersing it in the canning kettle full of hot water. Pack jars with cold raw fruit or partially cooked hot food.

   To pack fruits cold (except tomatoes), fill jars with raw fruit; then ladle hot syrup into jars, filling each to within ½ inch of jar rim.

   To pack food hot, bring the syrup or other liquid to boiling in a large pan, add the prepared fruit pieces, and cook briefly as directed. Remove fruit from syrup and pack into jars; then pour over enough of the syrup to fill jars to within ½ inch of rims, or as directed in recipe.

Fill jars with syrup to within ½ inch of rims

6) Run a narrow spatula down between the food and the side of the jar to release any air bubbles. With a clean, damp cloth, carefully wipe the jar rim, for food on the rim may prevent sealing. Remove a lid from the hot water and place it on a jar. (If lids stick together, plunge them into cold water; then submerge them again in boiling water.) Screw the jar

ring band on by hand as tightly as you comfortably can. As each jar is filled, set it in the canning kettle filled with hot (not boiling) water.

Release air bubbles

7) When all jars are filled and in the canner, pour in enough boiling water from the teakettle, if needed, to submerge the jars at least 1 inch under the surface. Cover the canner, turn heat to high, and as soon as water starts to break the surface at a hard simmer, take off the cover, reduce heat, and start counting the time required for processing (see charts for individual fruit on pages 12–13), keeping water at a hard simmer. Keep water at a gentle boil for tomatoes and pears. A vigorous boil evaporates the water too fast and is not necessary because the temperature reached by a hard simmer is sufficient for safe canning. Taking off the canner cover helps keep the temperature at a simmer. (If canning at altitudes above 3,000 feet, add 2 minutes processing time for each additional 1,000 feet.)

If liquid is lost from jar during this process, do not open the jar and add more liquid unless you intend to process it again. Liquid loss will not cause spoilage.

8) Lift jars from the canner with a special jar lifter or tongs. Do not cool in the canner or food will overcook. Place jars on a cloth or board away from drafts but do not cover; cool completely. If you wish, remove the ring bands.

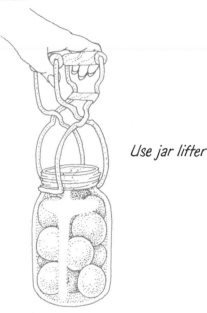

Use jar lifter

9) Test for a good seal by pressing the jar lid with your finger; if it stays down when pressed, the jar is sealed. Do not turn jar upside down to test for leaks because liquid could seep between the lid and jar top, breaking the seal. Label each jar and store in a cool, dry place.

Submerge jars at least 1 inch

Check lid for seal

Step-by-step canning for tomato juice

Use well-ripened tomatoes that are fresh, firm, and free of decayed spots. Check with your county cooperative extension service for high-acid varieties best for canning. Wash, peel, core, and cut into pieces. You can extract juice either from uncooked tomatoes or from those which have been heated just until soft. If you work with uncooked tomatoes, press out juice as soon as possible after they are cut so they will have minimum exposure to air. Or if you cook them, do it soon after cutting to inactivate the enzymes that change the consistency of the fruit and cause loss of vitamin C.

1) Get out canning jars, lids, and ring bands. Wash jars thoroughly. Check jars for nicks or cracks (see illustration, page 9) and discard. Also discard any rusted or bent ring bands. Wash and keep jars very hot until used. Also keep jar lids in very hot water until used. Then follow step 3, page 9.

2) Press either the uncooked or slightly cooked tomatoes through a fine colander or wire strainer to remove the seeds and smooth the texture. Add 1 teaspoon lemon juice or vinegar to each pint of juice (2 teaspoons for quarts) to prevent spoilage. Add salt to taste—about ½ teaspoon to each pint (1 teaspoon to quarts).

3) Heat the strained juice to the simmering point (204° F). Fill clean, hot jars one at a time with juice to within ¼ inch of top. With a clean, damp cloth, carefully wipe jar rim. Remove a lid from the hot water and place it on the jar. Screw the jar ring band on as tightly as you comfortably can. As each jar is filled, set it in the canning kettle filled with hot (not boiling) water that covers jars by 1 inch.

4) Finish canning the juice as directed in steps 7-9, page 10. Tomatoes change their texture and lose vitamin C during freezer storage and thawing. Tomato juice made from frozen tomatoes is thin and vitaminless.

Tomato-Vegetable Cocktail Juice

This mixture makes a healthful juice that can be served hot or cold.

15 pounds fully ripe tomatoes, coarsely chopped (you should have about 8 quarts)
2 cups celery, chopped
3 large onions, chopped
3 cloves garlic, minced or mashed
¼ cup sugar (or to taste)
2 tablespoons salt
¾ teaspoon pepper
2 teaspoons prepared horseradish
⅓ cup lemon juice
Worcestershire to taste

In at least a 10-quart kettle, combine the tomatoes, celery, onions, and garlic. Bring to boiling over medium-high heat and boil gently, stirring often, for about 20 minutes.

In a covered blender jar, whirl tomato mixture a small amount at a time until smooth. Press through a wire strainer, discarding pulp. Stir in the sugar, salt, pepper, horseradish, lemon juice, and Worcestershire.

You can chill the juice and pour it into freezer containers, cover, and freeze. Thin the juice before serving with broth if you like. Or can the juice.

To can, prepare 6 quart-sized canning jars, following step 1 on page 9 under Canning Fruits. Fill jars to within ¼ inch of rim. Then follow steps 7-9 on page 10, processing for 30 minutes. Makes 6 quarts.

Canning Guide for Fruit

Fruit and Varieties	To yield 1 pint (pounds)	Preparation for canning	Processing time (minutes)	
			pints	quarts
Apples Golden Delicious, Gravenstein, Jonathan, McIntosh, Newton Pippin, Winesap	1¼ to 1½ lbs.	*For pieces,* pare and remove cores; cut in slices or quarters; treat to prevent darkening. Cook in canning syrup or other liquid for 2 to 4 minutes; pack hot and cover with hot cooking liquid.	15	15
Applesauce		(see under Fruit purées and sauces on page 13)		
Apricots Blenheim (Royal), Tilton, Wenatchee Moorpark	1 to 1¼ lbs.	Peel as for peach, if desired. Cut in halves and remove pits or leave whole; treat for darkening. *To pack hot,* cook whole apricots in syrup or other liquid for 1 to 3 minutes; pack hot; cover with hot cooking liquid. *To pack raw,* fill jar with whole or halved apricots; cover with boiling syrup or liquid.	20 25	20 30
Bananas		Canning not recommended.		
Berries All berries except strawberries	¾ to 1½ lbs.	*For firm berries,* add about ½ cup sugar to 1 quart fruit in a pan; bring to boiling, shaking pan to prevent sticking; pack hot; cover with hot liquid. *For soft berries,* fill jar with raw fruit; shake down; cover with hot syrup or berry juice.	10 10	10 15
Sweet Cherries Bing, Black Tartarian, Chinook, Lambert, Napoleon (Royal Ann)	1 to 1½ lbs.	Pit, if desired; prick skins if left whole. *To pack hot,* bring cherries to boiling in syrup or other liquid; pack hot; cover with hot cooking liquid. *To pack raw,* pack fruit in jar; cover with boiling syrup or juice.	15 20	15 25
Figs Black Mission, Black Spanish (Brown Turkey), Calimyrna, Celeste, Granata, Kadota, Laterula	¾ to 1¼ lbs.	Bring to boiling in water or syrup; let stand 3 to 4 minutes. Pack hot in jar; add 1 tablespoon lemon juice per quart; cover with hot liquid or syrup.	90	90
Grapes	2 lbs.	Use ripe Muscat or slightly underripe Thompson seedless grapes for canning. Remove stems and wash. *To pack hot,* bring to a boil in a small amount of light or medium syrup. Pack hot into hot jars. Cover with the hot syrup. Seal. *To pack raw,* put into hot jars and cover with boiling syrup. Seal.	15 20	15 20
Grapefruit	2 lbs. (2 to 4 grape-fruit)	*To pack raw,* use thoroughly ripened fruit. Cut off peel including white membrane, lift out segment. Pack segments into jars. Cover with hot syrup.	30	35
Lemons and limes		Canning not recommended.		
Loquats	1½ to 2 lbs.	Remove stem and blossom ends; cut in half and remove seeds. Cook 3 to 5 minutes in syrup or other liquid. Pack hot; cover with boiling cooking liquid.	15	20

Fruit and Varieties	To yield 1 pint (pounds)	Preparation for canning	Processing time (minutes)	
			pints	quarts
Melons		Canning not recommended.		
Oranges		Canning not recommended.		
Peaches Alawar, Elberta, Gold Medal, J.H. Hale, Late Crawford, Redglobe, Redhaven, Rio Oso Gem, Rochester, Slappy, Valient, Veteran **Nectarines** Fire Globe, Freedom, Gold King, Gower, Late Grand, Le Grand, Marigold, Panamint, Rose, September Grand, Stanwick	1 to 1½ lbs.	Peel peaches by dipping in boiling water; plunge in cold water, then pull off skins. (Pare unevenly ripened peaches.) Pare nectarines if desired. Cut peaches and nectarines along seam, twist in half, and remove pits. Treat to prevent darkening (see page 8). *To pack hot,* heat in boiling syrup or other liquid until hot through; or, if fruit is juicy, add 1 cup sugar to 1 quart fruit and heat slowly just to boiling. Pack hot, then cover with hot syrup or cooking liquid. *To pack raw,* place fruit, cut side down, in jar; cover with boiling syrup or liquid.	(Freestone) 15 (Clingstone) 20 (Freestone) 20 (Clingstone) 25	20 20 25 30
Pears Bartletts best for canning	1 to 1½ lbs.	Pare, cut in halves, and remove cores; treat for darkening. *To pack hot,* cook in boiling syrup or other liquid just until heated through; pack hot and cover with hot syrup or cooking liquid. *To pack raw,* place fruit, cut side down, in jar; cover with boiling syrup or other liquid.	15 20	20 25
Persimmons Can as purée, Fuyu, Hachiya	1½ to 1¾ lbs.	Best canned as purée (see Fruit purées and sauces below).		
Plums and fresh prunes Duarte, El Dorado, Gaviota, Italian, Nubiana, President, Queen Ann, Santa Rosa, Standard, Stanley, Sugar, Wickson	1 to 1½ lbs.	Cut in halves and remove pits, or leave whole and prick skins. Peel if desired (as for peaches). *To pack hot,* drop fruit in syrup or juice; bring to boiling. Pack hot; cover with hot cooking liquid. *To pack raw,* put fruit in jar; cover with boiling syrup or juice.	15 20	15 20
Rhubarb	⅔ to 1 lb.	Cut ½-inch lengths. Add ½ to 1 cup sugar to 1 quart fruit; mix and let stand 3 or 4 hours. Bring to boiling; pack hot, then cover with hot juice.	10	10
Tomatoes Can as purée, pear-shaped tomatoes, yellow-fruited varieties, and large, firm, smooth tomatoes except beefsteak types	1¼ to 2¼ lbs.	Dip in boiling water, then dip in cold water; peel; cut out core. *To pack hot,* bring whole peeled tomatoes to boil in very small amount of juice or water. Pack hot, then cover with hot cooking liquid. Add 2 teaspoons lemon juice and 1 teaspoon salt to each quart. *To pack raw,* cut tomatoes in halves. Pack, cut side down, to the top, pressing down after each 2 tomatoes are packed. Add salt and lemon juice as above.	15 50	15 50
Fruit purées and sauces All purées except avocado	Amounts vary with fruits	If necessary, cook or steam fruits until soft in small amount of water. Mash fruit or press through wire strainer or whirl in a blender. Add sugar and/or lemon juice to taste. Heat until boiling and pack hot into jars.	20	25

Note: At altitudes above 3,000 feet, add 2 minutes processing time for each additional 1,000 feet.

Brandied Fruit Recipes

Canning fruits in brandy syrup gives them much the same flavor as fruits brandied the old-fashioned way, in a stone crock. And canning is a much more reliable method.

Apricots, cherries, peaches, pears, plums, and seedless grapes are all well suited for canning with brandy. They make delicious desserts served plain or topped with ice cream. They are also excellent meat accompaniments.

Each of the following recipes makes 6 pints of fruit. Prepare the 6 pint-sized canning jars and other canning equipment as directed in steps 1–3 on page 9. The varieties of fruit recommended for canning in the chart on pages 12–13 are the best for canning with brandy too. Because brandy displaces part of the syrup, you must use the more concentrated sugar syrups as directed in these recipes.

Apricots

1¼ cups sugar
1 cup water
6 to 8 pounds firm, ripe apricots
About 1¼ to 1½ cups brandy

For syrup, combine the sugar and water in a saucepan, bring to a boil, and cook until sugar dissolves; keep hot.

To prepare apricots, wash, cut in half, discard pits, and treat to prevent darkening (see information, page 8). Drain fruit and pack in hot jars, cavity sides down, firmly packing into jar. Pour in about ¼ cup hot sugar syrup. Pour on 3 to 4 tablespoons brandy (the amount depending on preference for a moderate or strong liqueur flavor). Add enough syrup to fill jars to within ½ inch of top. Proceed, following steps 6–10 on pages 9–10, processing jars 20 minutes. Makes 6 pints.

Sweet Cherries

Follow basic procedure as for Brandied Apricots, left. Wash 6 to 8 pounds cherries and remove pits, if desired. Use brandy, or substitute kirsch. Process pint jars 20 minutes.

Grapes

Follow basic procedure as for Brandied Apricots, left. Wash 6 to 8 pounds Thompson seedless grapes and remove stems. Process pint jars 15 minutes.

Peaches

Follow basic procedure as for Brandied Apricots, left. Select 6 to 8 pounds peaches. Dip fruit into scalding water for ½ to 1 minute to loosen skin; immediately plunge into cold water. When cool, peel, halve, and remove pits, and treat fruit to prevent darkening (see information on page 8). Process pint jars 25 minutes.

Pears

Follow basic procedure as for Brandied Apricots, left. Use 6 to 8 pounds pears. Peel, halve, cut out cores, and treat to prevent darkening (see information on page 8). Process pint jars 25 minutes.

Plums

Follow basic procedure as for Brandied Apricots, left. Choose 6 to 8 pounds plums. Wash, peel, cut in half, and pit. Process pint jars 20 minutes.

Jams and Other Preserves

Nothing is quite so tasty as homemade preserves spread on crisp toast or steaming hot biscuits to start the morning off right. Most preserves are easy to make, and the canning process is much simpler than for fruit canning.

You can use your culinary imagination to "put up" homemade sweets that are quite different from any you can buy at the store. Their distinctive flavors will enhance all your meals.

To achieve these delights, start by choosing the freshest fruits available.

"Preserves" have many tastes... many names

Fruits combined with sugar—usually boiled together—make the various types of preserves we enjoy. Don't let nomenclature confuse you; preserves fall under many names: jams, jellies, butters, conserves, and one called just "preserves" (see below). To get a good flavor and consistency, you need the right proportions of fruit, sugar, pectin, and acid. Some fruits have enough pectin and acid to jell when cooked with sugar; others require the addition of pectin or an acid, like lemon juice, or both. And sometimes fruits low in either acid or pectin are combined with other fruits that supply them in the right proportions.

Jams are combinations of crushed or chopped fruit and sugar that are cooked to a fairly smooth consistency, thick enough to spread well. Berries and soft fruits make good jams. Sometimes pectin and acid are added, depending on the fruit and the result desired. With commercial pectin, *a short-boiling method* is used and more sugar is required. **Always follow the directions on the package of pectin you are using, since directions are not interchangeable from one brand to another.** (For No-cook jams, see pages 66-67).

Jellies are fruit juices cooked with sugar. Good jelly should have transparent, bright color. When cut, it quivers but holds its shape. You start by extracting the juice and then straining it to make clear and sparkling jelly (this process is explained under Jellies, page 27). To make jellies of just the right consistency, it is especially important to have the right proportions of sugar, fruit, pectin, and acid.

Preserves are similar to jams, except that whole fruits or large pieces are used and they are cooked in such a way that the fruit retains its shape. The syrup that surrounds them should be bright and clear and have a good spreading consistency.

Marmalades are soft jellies, usually containing thin, suspended pieces of citrus peel or fruit.

Conserves are like jam, except that usually two or more fruits are cooked together. Often they contain raisins and nuts.

Butters are simply fruit purées that are combined with sugar and cooked down slowly to a thick, spreading consistency. Less sugar is used in making them than in making most other preserves, and often spices are added for flavor.

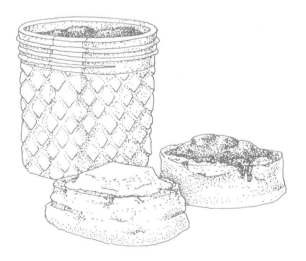

What equipment is needed?

You will need a cooking pot large enough to boil the fruit and sugar rapidly without their boiling over—one with a wide, flat bottom. An 8 to 10-quart pan is about right for most recipes.

Unless you plan to use up the preserves in a few weeks or to freeze them, they should be "put up" in regular canning jars (that can withstand the heat of boiling water) and covered with lids that can be sealed. (Hard-to-work-with paraffin alone will not prevent jam and jelly spoilage in hot, dusty, humid areas.) To facilitate unmolding of jelly, use small, straight-sided canning jars. As with any canning, do not use jars that are chipped or cracked.

An accurate thermometer is helpful in testing for doneness.

Step-by-step canning for jams, marmalades, preserves, conserves

1) Wash and sort fruit. You can leave fruit whole, chop, slice, and remove core, seeds, and skin as indicated in individual recipes. Do not use overripe fruit.

2) Get out canning jars, lids, and ring bands. Check jar rims for any nicks or cracks; dis-carding them (see illustration on page 9). Discard rusted or bent ring bands. Sterilize jars by placing them in boiling water for 15 minutes and keep hot. Scald lids and ring bands. Keep lids in very hot water until ready to use.

3) In the cooking pot, cook fruits in small batches as required in each recipe. Do not try to double recipes; it doesn't work.

4) Stir frequently while cooking, bringing fruit and its syrup to a quick boil. Watch that it doesn't boil over; this can happen quickly. Cook until thickened.

5) Pour into hot jars, spoon off any foam, and add more fruit to within 1/8 to 1/4 inch of top, depending on recipe. Wipe rims with a clean, damp cloth. Place lids on jars and screw on ring bands as tight as you comfortably can. Let cool on a towel out of a draft; then press lids with your finger. If they stay down, they're sealed (see illustration on page 10).

Jam Recipes

Strawberry-Rhubarb Jam

Rhubarb and strawberries combine well because the rhubarb takes on the flavor of the strawberry.

    1 pound rhubarb
    ¼ cup water
      About 4 cups full ripe strawberries
    6½ cups sugar
    1 pouch (3 oz.) or ½ bottle (6 oz.-size) liquid pectin

Thinly slice the unpeeled rhubarb and place in a saucepan; add water; cover pan and simmer until rhubarb is soft—about 1 minute—stirring once or twice. Measure rhubarb. Thoroughly crush strawberries and add enough strawberries to rhubarb to make 3½ cups fruit. (Pack fruit solidly into the cup to measure.) Turn the 3½ cups prepared rhubarb-strawberry mixture into a large saucepan. Add sugar and stir until dissolved.

Meanwhile, prepare 4 pint-sized jars, following step 2 on page 16.

Bring mixture to a full rolling boil, and stirring constantly, boil hard for 1 minute. Remove from heat and immediately stir in pectin. Skim off foam with a metal spoon. Stir mixture for 5 minutes

to cool slightly and to prevent floating fruit, occasionally skimming off foam. Proceed according to step 5 above. Makes 4 pints.

Raspberry-Plum Jam

Raspberries make delicious jam, but in the quantities needed to prepare jam, you may find them rather expensive. Extend the berries by combining them with more plentiful Santa Rosa plums to make this berry-flavored jam.

      About 2½ pounds Santa Rosa plums
    2 packages (about 10 oz. each) frozen
        raspberries in syrup (thawed) or 3 cups
        fresh raspberries
    10 cups sugar
    ½ cup lemon juice
    2 pouches (3 oz. each) or 1 bottle (6 oz.) liquid pectin

Prepare 6 pint-sized canning jars, following step 2 above.

Cut plums in half, remove pits, and finely chop or force through fine blade of a food chopper (you should have about 4 cups). Place plums and raspberries in an 8-quart kettle. Add sugar and lemon juice; stir until blended.

Over high heat, bring mixture to boiling, stirring constantly; boil 1 minute. Remove from heat; stir in pectin at once. Skim off foam and discard. Proceed according to step 5 on page 16, filling jars to within 1/8 inch of rim. Makes 6 pints.

Easy Raspberry Jam

This simple jam will please you because it cooks in such a short time.

    3 cups raspberries
    3 cups sugar

Prepare 3 half-pint-sized canning jars, following step 2 on page 16.

Mash berries in a saucepan and stir in sugar. Bring to a boil and boil for 3 minutes. Remove from heat and beat with a wire whip or rotary beater for 6 minutes. Proceed according to step 5 on page 16. Makes 3 half pints.

Trail Jam

To make fresh berry jam while on a camping trip, you'll need sugar and lemons; a stick of cinnamon is a flavorful option. Our recipe suits any tart berry, such as wild blackberries, raspberries, huckleberries, or blueberries; or purchase fresh tart berries locally. You can spread the jam on reflector oven biscuits, grilled toast, or use it to top pancakes.

In a pan combine 1 cup tart berries, ⅔ cup sugar, 1 tablespoon lemon juice, and 1 whole cinnamon stick (optional). Over a brisk fire boil fruit, stirring until it reaches desired thickness. Serve warm or cooled. Makes about 1¼ cups.

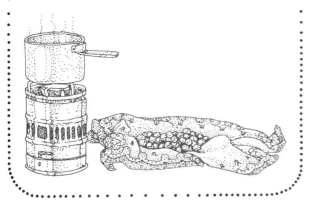

Old-Fashioned Strawberry Jam

When you make strawberry jam in 1-quart batches, it's easier to handle and cooks down more rapidly than in larger amounts. This basic, old-fashioned jam has a fresh berry flavor and is a clear, bright red.

    4 cups crushed fresh strawberries
    4 cups sugar

Prepare 2 pint-sized canning jars, following step 2 on page 16.

Stir the strawberries and sugar together in a large, 2 to 3-quart saucepan. Bring to a boil, stirring until the sugar dissolves. Keep at a moderate rolling boil for 10 to 15 minutes, or until thick. Then follow step 5 on page 16. Makes 2 pints.

Pumpkin-Orange Jam

Pumpkin mellows the orange in this brightly colored jam. It has a deliciously different taste and is so easy to prepare that you may decide to make some for holiday gifts.

    2 medium-sized oranges
    2 cups sugar
    4 cups pumpkin, canned or cooked

Grate outer layer of orange peels, remove and discard the inner white skin of the orange and then grind the pulp. Combine peel, pulp, and juice with sugar and pumpkin in a saucepan. Bring to a boil and simmer, uncovered, for 30 minutes.

Meanwhile, prepare 7 half-pint-sized canning jars, following step 2 on page 16. Proceed according to step 5. Makes 7 half pints.

Bing Cherry Jam

We suggest using Bings for this taste treat though Black Republican and Lambert are both acceptable substitutes. Use the jam on hot breads or toast. It is particularly good as a topping for any kind of cheesecake, thin dessert pancakes, cheese blintzes with sour cream, and vanilla or nut-flavored ice cream.

The simplest way to pit cherries is to use a cherry pitter, if you have one. But with jams, preserving the whole shape of the fruit is not essential, so you can gouge out pits with a clean paper clip, unbent to form an "S" shape. Or you may find it easier and faster to cut around each cherry to the pit, twist halves to free one side, and cut out pit with knife tip.

4 cups pitted ripe Bing cherries
3 cups sugar
2 tablespoons lemon juice
¼ teaspoon salt

Prepare 3 half-pint-sized canning jars, following step 2 on page 16.

Gently mix together in a large deep pan the cherries, sugar, lemon juice, and salt. Bring to a boil over medium heat, stirring constantly. Turn heat to high and cook rapidly, stirring frequently, for about 15 minutes or until liquid looks slightly thickened (it thickens considerably more when cooled). Proceed according to step 5 on page 16. Makes 3 half pints.

Honeydew Jam

Honeydew melon makes an outstanding carrier for the flavor of candied ginger in this jam.

3 cups honeydew melon pieces
3 cups sugar
3 tablespoons lemon juice
1 tablespoon chopped candied ginger

Combine in a pan the melon pieces, sugar, lemon juice, and candied ginger. Let stand until a syrup forms (about 2 hours). Bring to a boil and boil for 2 minutes, stirring constantly. Reduce heat and simmer, stirring frequently, until the mixture is thickened and the melon is translucent (about 45 minutes). Prepare 4 half-pint-sized canning jars, following step 2 on page 16. Proceed according to step 5. Makes 4 half pints.

Blueberry-Loganberry Jam

Loganberry wine sparks up this rich, colorful jam.

1 package (10 oz.) frozen blueberries,
    unsweetened
4 cups sugar
2 cups loganberry wine
2 tablespoons frozen orange juice concentrate
2 pouches (3 oz. each) or 1 bottle (6 oz.) liquid pectin

Prepare 7 half-pint-sized jars, following step 2 on page 16.

Mash thawed blueberries. Mix with sugar, wine, and orange juice. Cook over high heat, stirring to dissolve sugar. Bring to a boil and let boil very hard for 1 minute, stirring constantly. Remove mixture from heat and pour in pectin. Stir and skim for 6 minutes. Proceed according to step 5 on page 16. Makes 7 half pints.

Cranberry-Orange Jam

If you prefer a smooth cranberry jelly, pour the boiling hot jam through a small, sterilized wire strainer when you fill the jars.

1 pound cranberries
3 cups water
¾ cup orange juice
¼ cup lemon juice
4 cups sugar
2 pouches (3 oz. each) or 1 bottle (6 oz.) liquid pectin

Prepare 3 pint-sized canning jars following step 2 on page 16.

Sort through the cranberries and rinse well. Place cranberries and water in a 5-quart kettle and bring to a boil. Reduce heat and simmer, uncovered, for 10 minutes. Drain well, reserving water. Turn berries into a blender; whirl until puréed (bits of skin will remain; strain later if desired). Add enough of the reserved water to the berries to total 4 cups. Return cranberries to the kettle and stir in the orange juice, lemon juice, and sugar.

Over high heat, bring mixture to boiling, stirring constantly; boil, uncovered, 1 minute. Remove from heat; stir in pectin at once. Skim off and discard foam. Proceed according to step 5 on page 16, filling jars to within ⅛ inch of rim. Store at least 1 week before using. Makes 3 pints.

Huckleberry Jam

When you pick more berries than you can use fresh, you'll want to can or freeze them for later use. This jam can make an attractive and appreciated Christmas gift.

    6 cups crushed huckleberries
    1 package (2 oz.) powdered pectin
    8 cups sugar

Prepare 9 half-pint-sized canning jars, following step 2 on page 16.

Wash and drain the berries; put through a food chopper or whirl in the blender until the berries are crushed. Measure 6 cups of the crushed fruit into a large (6-quart) pan. (If you do not have quite enough fruit, add water to fill the last fraction of a cup.) Stir in the pectin and bring to a boil, stirring constantly. Add the sugar and continue stirring until the mixture comes to a full rolling boil. Let the fruit boil exactly 2 minutes. Remove from heat and skim off the foam. Proceed according to step 5 on page 16. Makes 9 half pints. *Note:* To use a 1 3/4-ounce package of pectin instead of the 2-ounce size, make this change: After adding sugar, boil jam just 1 minute, stirring constantly.

Plum Jam

Plums that have lots of sweet-tart flavor, such as Santa Rosa, are especially good for plum jam.

Wash plums and remove pits; put plums through a food chopper, using the coarse blade, to make 4 cups plums. Combine plums and 3½ cups sugar in a saucepan; let stand 1 hour.

Prepare 2 pint-sized canning jars, following step 2 on page 16. Place jam over low heat and cook, stirring frequently, until thickened. Then proceed according to step 5. Makes 2 pints.

Preserve Recipes

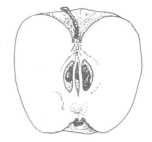

Apricot Butter

At the height of the apricot season, you may find you have an abundance of fresh apricots on hand. One solution is to make them into apricot purée. It is the quickest way to use large quantities of apricots in a hurry. Then, later make into Apricot Butter.

Use this recipe as an excellent topping for ice cream, delicious filling for cake, or a tasty spread for toast.

    1 quart apricot purée (directions follow)
    3 cups sugar
    2 tablespoons lemon juice

Prepare 5 half-pint-sized canning jars, following step 2, page 16.

Combine purée with sugar and lemon juice in a large saucepan and bring to a boil; cook rapidly, stirring, until thickened (about 15 to 18 minutes). Proceed with step 5 on page 16. Makes 5 half pints.

To make apricot purée. Wash and pit ripe apricots; whirl a few at a time in a blender or put through the fine blade of a food chopper to make a smooth purée. Expect to get 1 quart of purée from about 3 pounds ripe apricots. Add 2 tablespoons lemon juice to each quart of purée, or use ascorbic acid preparation, following the directions on the label to prevent darkening. (For freezing, pour purée into freezer containers, leaving about an inch head space.)

Apple Butter with Port

In a heavy 4 or 5-quart saucepan, combine 1 bottle (4/5 qt.) Port with 4 cups water and bring to a boil over high heat. Pare and thinly slice 8 large Golden Delicious apples (you should have 8 cups), add to wine mixture, and simmer uncovered, stirring occasionally, for 45 minutes.

Add 1½ cups sugar, ¼ teaspoon salt, ½ teaspoon ground cinnamon, and 1 whole stick cinnamon. Cook over medium-low heat, stirring frequently, until about as thick as hot applesauce (about 20 to 25 minutes longer).

Meanwhile, prepare 3 pint-sized canning jars,

following step 2 on page 16. Then proceed with step 5. Makes 3 pints.

Apricot-Pineapple Butter

A deliciously tart flavor with just a hint of pineapple taste characterizes this fruit butter. Surprisingly, it uses the apricot pits too.

4 quarts pitted, halved ripe apricots
12 apricot pits
1 cup water
5 cups sugar
2 cups canned, crushed pineapple (do not drain)

Prepare 5 pint-sized canning jars, following step 2 on page 16.

Cook together slowly in a large saucepan the apricots, pits, and water for 1 hour and 15 minutes, stirring occasionally. Press through a food mill (not pits). Cook strained pulp over low heat for 10 to 15 minutes more; add sugar and pineapple. Heat to boiling. Proceed with step 5 on page 16. Makes 5 pints.

Caramel Spice Pear Butter

There's extra flavor richness in this pear butter; it's contributed by the spices and some caramelized sugar.

About 15 Bartlett pears
2 cups water
6 cups sugar
1 teaspoon ground cloves
1½ teaspoons ground cinnamon
½ teaspoon ground ginger
2 tablespoons lemon juice

Wash the pears but do not peel or core them; slice into a heavy saucepan—at least 5-quart size. Add water, cover, and cook until tender (about 30 minutes).

Remove from heat and press the pears through a colander or a food mill; measure the pear pulp (you should have 8 cups) and return to the pan. Using a frying pan, heat 1½ cups of the sugar, stirring, until it melts and caramelizes to a medium brown color. Pour immediately into the pear pulp (the syrup will sizzle and harden, but dissolve again as the preserves cook). Add the remaining sugar, cloves, cinnamon, and ginger. Cook uncovered, until thick (about 45 minutes). Stir frequently as it begins to thicken to prevent

it from sticking; stir in lemon juice just before removing it from heat.

Meanwhile, prepare 9 half-pint-sized canning jars, following step 2 on page 16. Then proceed with step 5, filling jars to within ¼ inch of the rim. Makes 9 half pints.

Spiced Quinces and Orange Slices

8 quinces
4 cups water
2 cups cider vinegar
6 cups sugar
3 whole, medium-sized oranges, sliced thinly
3 sticks cinnamon, broken into 1-inch pieces
About 30 whole cloves
⅛ teaspoon salt

Wash quinces, remove cores, and peel. Place cores and peels in a saucepan with the 4 cups water. Cut quinces into quarters and place in another container with about 1 inch additional water in bottom (at least 1½ cups); cover. Simmer contents of both containers until quinces are tender; drain water from quinces. Strain juice from peels and cores, measure 1½ cups, and add to quinces. Add vinegar, sugar, orange slices (halved), cinnamon, cloves, and salt. Cook together over medium heat, stirring occasionally, until syrup is clear and slightly thickened.

Meanwhile, prepare 4 pint-sized canning jars, following step 2 on page 16. Then proceed with step 5. Makes 4 pints.

Ginger Apple Preserves

You'll be able to enjoy this preserve with meat or with your morning muffin or toast.

In a heavy 4 or 5-quart saucepan, combine 5 cups sugar with 2 cups water. Bring to a boil over high heat. Reduce heat to medium and boil, uncovered, for 10 to 15 minutes. Meanwhile, pare 8 or 9 large, tart apples (Pippins, Jonathans, Winesaps) and cut into ¼-inch slices (you should have about 8 cups); sprinkle with 2 tablespoons lemon juice and mix well. Drain 1 jar (about 5 oz.) preserved ginger, reserving syrup, and chop (you should have about ½ cup).

Add apples, ginger, and reserved syrup to sugar-water mixture and boil gently, stirring occasionally, for 35 to 40 minutes or until preserve is thickened and apples are translucent.

Meanwhile, prepare 3 pint-sized canning jars, following step 2 on page 16. Then proceed with step 5, filling jars to within ⅛ inch of rim. Makes 3 pints.

Conserve Recipes

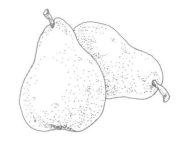

Fresh Fig Conserve

Black Mission figs give an especially attractive red color to this conserve.

2½ **pounds fresh figs**
2½ **cups sugar**
⅓ **cup lemon juice**
1 **tablespoon grated orange peel**
¼ **cup chopped walnuts**

Clip the stems from the figs and chop. Combine the figs and sugar in a large pan (about 5-quart size) and allow to stand for 1 hour. Place over medium heat and cook, stirring often, until thickened (about 20 minutes). Add the lemon juice, orange peel, and walnuts. Bring to boiling again; boil for 3 minutes.

Meanwhile, prepare 5 half-pint-sized canning jars, following step 2 on page 16. Then proceed with step 5. Makes 5 half pints.

Pear and Apricot Conserve

In this colorful conserve, pear, apricot, and lemon each asserts a distinct character without disturbing the harmonious blend. The pears contribute their delicate flavor, the apricots their bright color, and the lemon its tartness.

1 **cup (about 6 oz.) dried apricots, cut into thin slices**
1 **whole lemon, thinly sliced and seeds removed (ends discarded)**
1 **cup water**
5 **cups peeled, cored, and chopped firm-ripe Anjou or Bosc pears (about 5 large)**
4 **cups sugar**

In a small pan, combine apricots, lemon, and water; bring to a boil and then simmer, uncovered, for 5 minutes; set aside.

In a 5-quart or larger saucepan, combine the pears and sugar; cook, stirring occasionally, until sugar dissolves and mixture boils. Boil gently, uncovered, stirring occasionally, for 25 minutes. Add cooked apricot mixture and boil, uncovered,

another 5 minutes or until reduced to about 5 cups.

Meanwhile, prepare 5 half-pint-sized canning jars, following step 2 on page 16. Then proceed with step 5, filling jars to within ⅛ inch of rim. Makes 5 half pints.

Rhubarb Conserve

You let the rhubarb and sugar blend overnight; then proceed with the conserve. Raisins and dates add extra sweetness. You can serve it on toast, with meats, or as an ice cream topping.

2½ **pounds rhubarb, diced (about 4 cups)**
2½ **pounds sugar (about 5½ cups)**
2 **whole oranges**
1 **whole lemon**
1½ **cups each seedless raisins and chopped dates**
1 **cup chopped walnuts**

Wash rhubarb; cut off leaf and root ends, and dice. Place rhubarb and sugar in a large saucepan; cover and let stand overnight.

Cut the oranges and lemon into thin slices; then cut each slice into small pieces. Add orange and lemon pieces with dates and raisins to rhubarb-sugar mixture. Bring to a boil and, stirring occasionally, simmer until thickened (about 35 to 40 minutes). Add the walnuts about 5 minutes before removing from heat.

Meanwhile, prepare 5 pint-sized canning jars, following step 2 on page 16. Then proceed with step 5. Makes 5 pints.

Peach-Pineapple-Orange Conserve

These three familiar fruits combine to make a tangy preserve similar to marmalade. You can serve it with toast, or with ham or poultry.

8 to 10 medium-sized ripe peaches
2 medium-sized oranges
1 can (about 9 oz.) crushed pineapple (undrained)
6 cups sugar

Peel and pit the peaches and put through the food chopper, using a medium blade; catch all the peach juices and measure (you should have 4 cups peach pulp and juice). Wash oranges but do not peel. Cut into sections and remove any seeds; then put through the food chopper. In a large, heavy pan (at least 6-quart size), combine the peach and orange pulp; add the crushed pineapple and sugar. Cook on medium-low heat, stirring frequently, until thickened (about 35 minutes).

Meanwhile, prepare 5 pint-sized canning jars, following step 2 on page 16. Then proceed with step 5. Makes 5 pints.

Sunshine Preserves

Some of our grandparents used to make preserves by harnessing the radiant energy of the summer sun. The method is just as effective today. Apricot halves, nectarine and peach slices, and whole berries—such as blackberries, blueberries, currants, and raspberries—swell to plumpness and retain their shapes when cooked in this gentle manner.

You begin the process on the range, heating fruit and sugar together until the sugar dissolves. Cool the mixture slightly; then pour it into wide, shallow pans or trays of glass, metal, rigid plastic, or foil. Except for an opening to permit evaporation, the pans are covered with plastic film or glass, which concentrates the heat of the sun somewhat like a lens and protects the preserves from insects or falling leaves.

Next, arrange the pans in full sun on a table or rack. Preserves need frequent stirring during the time it takes for them to thicken. How long that is depends on your sun. In two of Sunset's tests, it took 10 hours in Seattle, and just 2 hours in Phoenix.

Sunshine Preserves retain remarkably fresh fruit flavor and are, indeed, less sweet than more conventional recipes. Although they are at their very best when eaten still warm from the sun, the preserves can also be refrigerated, frozen, or sealed in tempered glass canning jars for use later.

Sunshine Apricot Preserves

About 2 pounds firm, ripe apricots
3 cups sugar
2 tablespoons lemon juice

Wash apricots and cut fruit into halves or quarters; discard pits. Measure 4 cups of the fruit and combine with the sugar and lemon juice in a 4 or 5-quart saucepan; stir gently to mix. Cover and let stand at room temperature for 1 hour. Over medium heat, bring mixture to boiling, stir-

ring constantly. Turn heat to high and boil vigorously, uncovered, for 4 minutes without stirring. Remove pan from heat and let cool, uncovered, for 30 minutes.

Pour mixture into shallow glass or metal baking pans, roasting pans made of foil, or rigid plastic trays so that the syrup around the fruit is at least ⅓ inch deep but no deeper than ¾ inch. Cover with clear plastic film or a sheet of glass, leaving a 1-inch-wide opening along one side. Place pan in direct sunlight. Gently stir mixture and turn fruit pieces over every hour.

Remove preserves from sun when fruit is plump and syrup is thickened to about the consistency of corn syrup; the preserves thicken slightly more as they cool. It will take about 2 to 10 hours, or more, depending on the heat of the sun. You may need to bring the preserves in at night and then return to the sun the following day. Serve at once or store according to directions that follow. Makes 3 cups.

Peach or nectarine preserves. Cut peeled peaches or peeled or unpeeled nectarines into ½-inch-thick slices; discard pits. Follow Apricot Preserve recipe but increase lemon juice to ¼ cup.

Berry preserves. For whole blackberries, blueberries, boysenberries, currants, gooseberries, raspberries, and strawberries (stems removed), follow the Apricot Preserve recipe above.

How To Store Sunshine Preserves

Store uneaten preserves by one of the following methods: Spoon preserves into jars and cover; when refrigerated they will keep for at least 4 weeks. Or pack into freezer containers to within 1 inch of top, seal, and freeze.

To can preserves, prepare 3 half-pint-sized canning jars, following step 1 on page 9. Then proceed with steps 3 and 5–9, page 10, processing for 10 minutes. Makes 3 half pints.

Marmalade Recipes

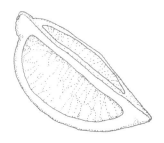

Bittersweet Marmalade

Because this recipe uses the whole peel from a combination of oranges, grapefruit, and lemons, it's both sharp and tart.

> **6 medium-sized, thin skinned oranges**
> **2 each lemons and medium-sized grapefruit, both with thin skins**
> **2 cups water**
> **9 cups sugar**

Cut the whole oranges, lemons, and grapefruit into ⅛-inch slices, discarding seeds and end pieces. Cut the orange and lemon slices in quarters and cut grapefruit slices in eighths. In a 6-quart or larger heavy pan, combine the oranges, lemons, grapefruit, and water. Bring to boiling; then cover and simmer until peel is tender when pierced and translucent in appearance (about 25 to 30 minutes).

Add sugar to the pan and stir until it dissolves. Increase heat to medium-high and cook, uncovered, stirring often as mixture thickens. Boil until the jell point is reached (see information on page 26). This will take about 30 minutes. Cover and let stand at room temperature for 18 to 24 hours.

Prepare 8 pint-sized canning jars, following step 2 on page 16.

Rapidly return marmalade to boiling, stirring to prevent sticking. Then proceed with step 5 on page 16, filling jars to within ⅛ inch of tops. Makes 8 pints.

Lemon Marmalade

This lemon marmalade uses only the thin yellow part of the peel to make a preserve that is especially fresh and tart tasting with scarcely any bitterness.

> **About 11 medium-sized lemons**
> **½ cup water**
> **6 cups sugar**
> **1 pouch (3 oz.) or ½ bottle (6 oz.-size) liquid pectin**

Use a small sharp knife to slice off all the thin outer yellow peel from lemons; cut peel into slivers. Then ream the juice from the lemons. You should have 1¾ cups peel and 2 cups lemon juice. Combine the peel, water, and ½ cup of the lemon juice in a 3-quart or larger saucepan. Bring to boiling; then cover and simmer until peel is tender when pierced (about 25 minutes).

Add remaining lemon juice and the sugar to the pan; cook, stirring, until sugar dissolves. Then turn heat high and bring to a full rolling boil. Remove from heat, cover, and let stand at room temperature for 18 to 24 hours.

Prepare 4 half-pint-sized jars, following step 2 on page 16.

Rapidly return marmalade to boiling, stirring to prevent sticking. Stir in the pectin and boil, stirring constantly, for exactly 1 minute. Quickly skim off any foam that forms. Follow step 5 on page 16, filling jars to within ⅛ inch of top. Makes 4 half pints.

Pear Marmalade

The flavor of pears dominates, but three other fruits add sparkle and color to these interesting, attractive preserves.

> **About 4 pounds firm, ripe pears**
> **1 large can (1 lb. 14 oz.) sliced pineapple**
> **2 large seedless oranges**
> **About 12 cups sugar**
> **1 small jar (4 oz.) maraschino cherries**

Peel pears, remove cores, and slice thinly; cut each slice into about 4 pieces; you should have 2 quarts. Drain the canned pineapple and cut each slice into about ¼-inch pieces. Cut the orange, including the peel, into thin slices, then cut each slice into about 4 wedges.

Combine the fruits and add sugar; mix and let stand overnight.

The next day, turn into a large kettle and bring to a boil; then reduce heat and boil it gently, stirring occasionally, until the fruit begins to look translucent (about 1 hour). Drain the maraschino cherries and cut each cherry into small pieces; add to the other fruits.

Meanwhile, prepare 5 pint-sized canning jars, following step 2 on page 16. Then proceed with step 5. Makes 5 pints.

Note: You can also make this marmalade with firm, ripe peaches (when in season) instead of the pears.

Spicy Tomato Marmalade

4 to 5 pounds fully ripe tomatoes
1 each orange and lemon
¼ cup cider vinegar
1½ teaspoons each ground cinnamon and allspice
¾ teaspoon ground cloves
3 cups sugar

Peel, core, and coarsely chop the tomatoes (you should have 8 cups). With a vegetable peeler, carefully remove thin outer peel from the orange and lemon; cut peel into thin slivers. Holding fruit over a bowl to catch the juice, cut remaining peel and white membrane off the orange and lemon and discard; coarsely chop the fruit.

In a 5-quart Dutch oven, combine the tomatoes, orange, lemon, slivered peel, vinegar, cinnamon, allspice, cloves, and sugar. Bring to boiling, reduce heat, and simmer gently, uncovered, until reduced to about 2 pints; it takes about 2 hours. Stir frequently to prevent sticking.

Prepare 2 pint-sized canning jars, following step 2 on page 16. Then proceed with step 5, filling jars to within ⅛ inch of top. Makes 2 pints.

Rhubarb Marmalade

Tiny bits of citrus peel add a surprisingly refreshing flavor to this bright red rhubarb preserve.

2 pounds rhubarb, diced
2 pounds sugar (4½ cups)
   Juice and peel of 1 large orange
   Juice and peel of ½ lemon

Combine rhubarb and sugar and let stand overnight in a glass container.

The next day, add orange juice and lemon juice. With a food grinder, coarsely grind the orange and lemon peels and add to the rhubarb mixture. Simmer about 1½ hours or until the marmalade is sufficiently thick, stirring occasionally.

Prepare 2 pint-sized canning jars, following step 2 on page 16.

Proceed with step 5 on page 16. Makes 2 pints.

Marmalade in an Orange Shell

Sugar-frosted orange shells, filled with bittersweet orange marmalade, make handsome containers on the breakfast table; they keep well for several weeks in the refrigerator. When the marmalade is gone, you can slice and eat the shells.

Candied orange shells. Wash 4 large oranges and cut a ½-inch-thick lid off the stem of each. With a curved grapefruit knife, cut fruit away from the rind, scraping any remaining membrane away from rind with a heavy spoon. Scrape fruit pulp off lid. Cover shells and lids with cold water; bring to a boil and boil 10 minutes; drain. Repeat this process four times; cool shells.

In a 4-quart pan, combine 6 cups *each* water and sugar. Add 6 tablespoons glycerine (purchased from a drug store). Heat, stirring, until sugar is dissolved. Add shells and lids and bring to boil. Boil until syrup is medium thick (220° F on a candy thermometer). Let shells and lids stand in syrup 24 hours, turning them several times. Then bring syrup to a boil again and boil until syrup is thick (232° F), turning shells over several times to prevent scorching. Remove shells and lids from syrup; turn each upside down over an inverted paper cup to drain. Let cool enough to handle; roll in granulated sugar. Cool thoroughly. Fill; secure lid with picks.

Orange Marmalade

5 medium-sized whole oranges, or enough to make 4 cups
2 small whole lemons
3 cups water
6 cups sugar
½ cup lemon juice

Thinly slice the oranges and lemons, discarding seeds. Cover fruit with the water; let stand overnight. Bring to a boil and boil 40 minutes. Let stand 4 hours. Add sugar, bring to a boil, stirring constantly, and boil for 20 minutes, stirring occasionally (or until the mixture sheets off a spoon—220° F). Add the lemon juice.

Meanwhile, prepare 7 half-pint-sized canning jars, following step 2 on page 16. Then proceed with step 5. Makes 7 half pints.

Mandarin Marmalade

The distinctive, more-than-orange flavor of the mandarin is probably best emphasized in this marmalade. It has a bright, deep color and a very special taste.

5 or 6 Kinnow or Wilking mandarin oranges
3 cups water
4½ cups sugar

Carefully peel mandarins with your fingers, keeping pieces of peel as large as possible; set peel aside.

Cut mandarins in half crosswise; pick out seeds and discard. Whirl enough fruit in a blender (or rub through a food mill) to make 2 cups pulp; pour into a wide saucepan. Add water.

Very thinly slice (cut in julienne strips) enough of the mandarin peel to make ½ cup; add peel and sugar to pulp in pan. Stir over medium heat until sugar is dissolved. Turn heat to high and boil rapidly, stirring frequently, until the jell point is reached (see information on page 26). This takes about 40 minutes. Remove marmalade from heat at once.

Meanwhile, prepare 2 pint-sized canning jars, following step 2 on page 16. Then proceed with step 5. Makes 2 pints.

Jack-o'-Lantern in a Jar

Marmalade made with translucent bits of pumpkin mingled with orange and lemon has a flavor that's lighter and fresher than most all-citrus marmalades. You can use a leftover jack-o'-lantern, but do so while it's still fresh and firm. Cut the pumpkin in half and use a large metal spoon to scrape away soot, candle wax, and any remaining seeds. Wash and drain well; cut into chunks, wrap airtight, and refrigerate.

1 each medium-sized orange and lemon
3 cups water
About a 3-pound pumpkin
4 cups sugar

Thinly slice the unpeeled orange and lemon, discarding end pieces; cut slices into quarters. In a 4 or 5-quart heavy saucepan, combine the orange, lemon, and water. Bring to boiling, cover, and simmer until orange peel is tender when pierced (about 25 minutes).

Meanwhile, peel pumpkin and cut away blossom and stem ends. Cut into strips about ½ inch wide and ⅛ inch thick; then cut strips into ½-inch squares (you should have 2 quarts pumpkin).

Add sugar to the pan; cook and stir until it dissolves. Add the pumpkin, turn heat to high, and cook rapidly (uncovered), stirring often as mixture thickens. Cook until the jell point is reached (see information on page 26); it takes about 40 minutes. Cover and let stand at room temperature for 18 to 24 hours.

Prepare 2 pint-sized canning jars, following step 2 on page 16.

Return marmalade to medium-high heat; bring to a full, rolling boil, stirring often to prevent the marmalade from sticking; boil for 1 minute.

Proceed with step 5 on page 16, filling jars to within ⅛ inch of jar tops. Makes 2 pints.

Quick Peach Marmalade

An interesting combination of large, fresh peaches and orange marmalade makes for a sweet-tart preserve.

6 large peaches (about 3 lbs.)
¼ cup lemon juice
7½ cups sugar
½ teaspoon butter or margarine
1 pouch (3 oz.) or ½ bottle (6 oz.-size) liquid pectin
1 jar (about 1 lb.) orange marmalade

Prepare 5 pint-sized canning jars, following step 2 on page 16.

Wash, peel, and pit peaches. Put through a food chopper, using a fine blade. Place peaches in a saucepan with lemon juice, sugar, and butter. Bring to a boil and boil for 1 minute, stirring constantly. Remove from heat; stir in liquid pectin and orange marmalade. Let cool, stirring occasionally, for 5 minutes. Then proceed with step 5 on page 16. Makes 5 pints.

Getting Jelly to Jell

Bright, transparent jelly is beautiful to look at and should be tender enough to spread and serve even as it holds its jiggly shape.

Jelly is made from fruit juice, extracted and cooked until the "jell point" is reached (see information below describing jell point). You'll need the proper amounts of fruit juice, pectin, acid, and sugar in order to make good jelly.

It is important to start with sound, ripe fruit. Underripe fruit contains more pectin than ripe fruit does, but ripe fruit is needed for full sweetness and flavor. For a list of the fruits that do or do not need added pectin or acid when making jelly, see the table below.

These fruits usually contain enough pectin and acid for jelly:

Apples, tart	Grapes, eastern Concord
Blackberries, tart	Lemons
Crabapples	Loganberries
Cranberries	Plums, most varieties
Currants	Prunes, sour
Gooseberries	Quince

These fruits usually are low in acid or pectin:

Apples, ripe	Grape juice, eastern
Blackberries, ripe	Concord
Cherries, sour	Grapes, California
Elderberries	Loquats
Grapefruit	Oranges

These fruits always need added acid or pectin, or both:

Apricots	Pears
Figs	Pomegranates
Grapes, western	Prunes
Concord	Raspberries
Guava	Strawberries
Peaches	

If you need extra pectin

One way to test the fruit juice you have at home to see how much pectin it has is to add 1 teaspoon of cooked fruit juice to 1 tablespoon rubbing alcohol (70 percent alcohol). Stir to mix—do not taste. Juices rich in pectin will form a jellylike mass that can be picked up with a fork. Juices low in pectin will form only a few pieces of jellylike material. If more pectin is needed, add a commercial pectin (liquid or powder form) or mix the juice with another fruit juice of higher pectin content. Discard alcohol test.

If pectin is to be added, add 1 tablespoon liquid pectin to 1 cup fruit juice. Test again for pectin. If more is needed, add another tablespoon of pectin and test again. Repeat until the test indicates that enough pectin has been added. Measure the remaining juice; add proper amount of pectin.

Testing for enough acid

A tart juice is necessary for a good-tasting jelly. Compare the tartness of the juice with a mixture of 1 teaspoon lemon juice added to 3 tablespoons water and ½ teaspoon sugar. If the juice is not as tart as the mixture, add 1 tablespoon lemon juice to each cup of fruit juice.

Finding the magic jell point

The easiest way to tell when jelly has reached the jell point is to use an accurate thermometer. When its temperature reaches 221° F, the jelly is ready. (This is at sea level. To test at your elevation, boil water to see at what temperature it boils; then add 8° F for the jelling point.)

If you have no thermometer, dip a cool metal spoon into the boiling juice. Lift it out and watch how the juice runs off the side of the spoon. When the juice has almost reached the jell point, the juice will slowly come together and fall off the spoon in two drops. When the drops run together and slide off the spoon in a sheet, the jelly is ready; remove from heat immediately.

Or you can put a little jelly on a plate in the refrigerator. If it jells in a few minutes, the jelly is ready. (Make sure to take the jelly off the heat while you make the test.)

Step-by-step canning for jelly

1) Get out canning jars, lids, and ring bands. Check jar rims for nicks or cracks; discard them (see illustration on page 9). Discard any rusted or bent ring bands. Place canning jars or jelly glasses in boiling water for 15 minutes to sterilize. Keep jars in hot water until ready to use. Scald lids and ring bands; keep lids in scalding hot water until used.

2) Wash ripe fruit, removing stems or spoiled parts. Do not core or peel apples or other firm fruits—cut them into small pieces or grind in a food chopper. If fruit is soft, crush it to start the juice flowing.

3) To extract the juice, put crushed or cut fruit into a pan. Add only enough water to prevent scorching, since the juice shouldn't be diluted any more than necessary. Firm fruit will need some water (add about ¼ cup water for each pound of semifirm fruit, such as plums, or about 1 cup water for each pound of very firm fruit, such as apples). Soft fruits usually don't need water, but overripe fruit often needs about ¼ cup water for each pound of fruit. Bring fruit to boil; boil rapidly until tender (10 to 20 minutes). Too much boiling reduces the jelling strength.

4) Pour fruit mixture through four thicknesses of wet, washed cheesecloth spread over a colander or into a regular jelly bag made of strong muslin. Twist bag and press out juice. To make very clear jelly, let juice drip without squeezing bag.

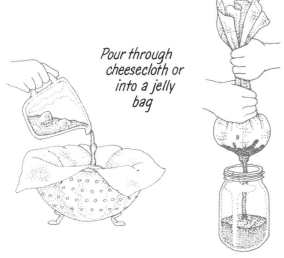

Pour through cheesecloth or into a jelly bag

5) You can use one of two methods to make jelly. *The short-boil method* depends on the use of a bottle or package of commercial pectin and uses a higher proportion of sugar. The boiling time, usually about 1 minute, cannot be varied from the package or recipe directions. Then continue on with step 6 below.

The longer-boil method uses a little less sugar. Unless you are following a recipe exactly, you'll need to test the juice for amount of natural fruit pectin and acid, supplying either or both if needed. (See page 26 for how to test and adjust for pectin and acid.)

Cook only 4 to 6 cups juice at a time, using a kettle that holds 4 to 5 times the amount of juice to be cooked (1 cup juice plus 1 cup sugar makes 1¼ cups jelly).

Follow recipe. Or if not using a recipe, combine juice with pectin or acid (if needed) and place over heat. (A small piece of butter added to the juice tends to keep it from boiling over and reduces foam.) The amount of sugar you use will depend on the pectin and acid content of the juice. If you don't have a recipe, a good general rule is to use about ¾ to 1 cup sugar for juice with a high proportion of pectin (or ⅔ to ¾ cup for juice containing only a moderate amount of pectin) to each cup of fruit juice.

When fruit juice comes to a boil, add the sugar and stir until dissolved. Boil rapidly until the jell point is reached (see page 26). Flavor, color, and jelling ability are lost if jelly is allowed to boil too long.

6) Remove jelly from heat immediately when time is up, if you use the short-boil method. Or remove it when the jell point is reached for the longer-boil method. Let stand a minute to allow foam to form; then carefully remove the foam. Pour hot jelly quickly into hot jars, filling jars to within about ⅛ inch of tops. Carefully wipe off rim of jar. Put lid on each jar as it is filled, screwing band on as tightly as you comfortably can. Cool jars away from drafts on a towel. To test for a good seal, see step 9 on page 10. Store in a cool, dark area.

Using Paraffin To Seal Jelly

By far the most reliable method of sealing preserves is to put them in regular canning jars with lids that seal. Paraffin can be used if jams and jellies are stored in a cool, dry place and used within a few months. (Changes in temperature may cause jelly to seep up around paraffin.)

To use paraffin, pour hot jelly into the hot jelly glasses to within ½ inch of the top instead of ⅛ inch as called for in regular canning jars that seal. Cover quickly with a thin layer of hot paraffin (about ⅛ inch thick). This thin layer will hold a good seal. Make sure the paraffin touches all sides of the glass by rotating the jar to expose the hot wax to the glass. Let glasses stand until the wax hardens, pricking any bubbles that form on the surface. Place the jelly caps on the jars.

Jelly Recipes

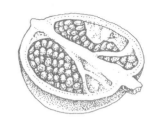

Lime Mint Jelly

Lime and mint together make an outstanding jelly. Since the combination isn't too sweet, it can be used as an accompaniment for any meat—but it's especially good with lamb.

    Grated peel of 5 limes
 ¾ cup lime juice
 4 cups sugar
 1¾ cups water
    Green food coloring
 1 pouch (3 oz.) or ½ bottle (6 oz.-size) liquid pectin
 3 tablespoons finely chopped mint leaves

Prepare 5 half-pint-sized canning jars, following step 1 on page 27.

Prepare the grated lime peel and set aside; squeeze out lime juice, using more limes (about 3) to make ¾ cup juice. Pour juice, sugar, and water into a large saucepan; mix well. Bring mixture to a boil; stir in enough food coloring to get the desired shade. Add pectin, stirring constantly. Blend in grated lime peel and chopped mint leaves. Boil vigorously for 30 seconds.

Then proceed with step 6 on page 27. Makes 5 half pints.

Note: To use the 1¾-ounce package of powdered pectin, follow above recipe but boil only 1 minute after adding sugar.

Pomegranate Jelly

For an easy way to remove seeds, cut the crown end off each pomegranate and lightly score the peel lengthwise down the sides in several places. Put the scored fruit in a bowl or sink of cold water and let soak at least 5 minutes. Holding the fruit under water, break sections apart with your fingers and separate the seeds from the pulp; as you work, the seeds sink to the bottom and the pulp and peel float. With a wire strainer, skim off the pulp.

Pomegranate juice. Whirl about 1½ to 2 cups pomegranate seeds at a time in a blender until liquefied. Pour through a cheesecloth-lined wire

strainer and let drain gradually. (Or to speed the straining, wear rubber gloves and press small amounts of seeds and juice at a time through the cheesecloth.) Store in refrigerator up to 5 days, or freeze for longer storage. One medium-sized pomegranate makes about ½ cup juice.

 3½ cups pomegranate juice, fresh or frozen, thawed (see above)
 ¼ cup lemon juice
 1 package (2 oz.) powdered pectin
 4½ cups sugar

Prepare 3 pint-sized canning jars, following step 1, page 27. In a large kettle, combine the pomegranate juice, lemon juice, and pectin. Over high heat, bring to a rolling boil, stirring constantly. Add the sugar and stir to blend; bring to a second rolling boil; then boil exactly 2 minutes.

Proceed with step 6 on page 27, filling jars to within ⅛ inch of rims. Makes 3 pints.

Loquat Jelly

 4 cups loquat juice (directions follow)
 ½ cup lemon juice
 1 package (2 oz.) powdered pectin
 5 cups sugar

Prepare 7 half-pint-sized canning jars, following step 1 on page 27.

In a large pan, combine the loquat juice, lemon juice, and pectin; bring to a full boil. Add the sugar all at once and bring to a full boil again, boiling hard for 2 minutes and stirring constantly. Proceed with step 6 on page 27. Makes 7 half pints.

Note: If using 1¾-ounce package pectin, make this change: After adding the sugar, boil 1 minute, stirring constantly.

Loquat juice. For each 2 to 3 cups juice, wash about 5 pounds whole loquats. Place in a large pan with 1 cup water and ½ cup lemon juice; cover and bring to a boil. Then cook over low heat about 40 minutes, stirring occasionally, until loquats are cooked to a sauce. Press out juices in a food mill or wire strainer, discarding seeds and pulp. Amount of juice yield varies with size of the fruit.

Quince Jelly

Juice from quince jells easily because it has a high pectin content. The jelly has quite a light, delicate flavor.

4 cups quince juice (directions follow)
3 cups sugar

Bring juice to a boil in a deep saucepan. Add sugar and stir until dissolved. Boil rapidly until mixture reaches jell point (see page 26).

Prepare 2 pint-sized canning jars, following step 1 on page 27. Proceed, according to step 5, using the longer-boil method; then proceed with step 6. Makes 2 pints.

Quince juice. Peel, core, and coarsely chop enough quince to make 8 cups. Put in a pan with 6 cups water. Bring to a boil and simmer gently for 45 minutes. Separate juice from fruit by pouring through a jelly bag or 4 layers of cheesecloth stretched and tied over the top of a deep bowl. Do not squeeze bag or jelly may be cloudy.

Huckleberry Jelly

8 cups huckleberries
1 cup water
2 tablespoons each orange juice and lemon juice
1 package (2 oz.) powdered pectin
4½ cups sugar

Prepare 6 half-pint-sized canning jars, following step 1 on page 27.

Combine the berries, water, orange juice, and lemon juice in a large pan. Bring to a boil and simmer 2 to 3 minutes; cool. Pour the fruit and juice through a muslin bag, squeezing the bag to release all the juice. Measure 3½ cups juice into large pan. (If you do not have quite enough juice, add water to fill the remaining fraction of a cup.) Stir in the pectin and bring to a boil, stirring constantly. Add the sugar and continue stirring until the mixture comes to a full rolling boil. Boil exactly 2 minutes. Remove from heat; skim off foam. Proceed with step 6 on page 27. Makes 6 half pints.

Note: If you use a 1¾-ounce package of pectin instead of the 2-ounce size, make this change: After adding sugar, boil jelly just 1 minute, stirring constantly.

Red Currant Jelly

4 cups currant juice (see below)
3 to 4 cups sugar

In a large deep saucepan, bring juice to a boil. Add the sugar (3 cups for a very tart jelly, 4 cups for a sweeter jelly) and stir until sugar dissolves. Boil rapidly until the mixture reaches the jell point (see page 26).

Meanwhile, prepare 3 pint-sized canning jars, following step 1 on page 27. Then proceed with step 6. Makes 3 pints.

Red currant juice. Stem, wash, and drain enough red currants to measure 4 quarts. Add 2 cups water and mash fruit very slightly. Bring to a boil and simmer gently for 10 minutes. Let juice drip through a jelly bag or a large wire strainer lined with a muslin cloth (dipped in cold water and wrung dry). For clear jelly, do not squeeze the cloth. Makes 5 to 6 cups.

Making Wine Jelly

The mellow wine flavors of these jellies complement both meats and cheeses.

The best wines for making jelly are those with a full natural flavor and body, although any wine may be used. Here are some suggestions: for a deep red jelly, try a mellow Port, such as Ruby Port, or a robust red table wine, such as Pinot Noir or Zinfandel. For a soft rosy jelly, pick a fruity Rosé wine, such as Grenache Rosé.

Wine Jelly

1¾ cups (4/5 pt.) wine
3 cups sugar
1 pouch (3 oz.) or ½ bottle (6 oz.-size) liquid pectin

Prepare 4 half-pint-sized canning jars or jelly glasses, following step 1 on page 27.

Mix wine and sugar in top of a double boiler. Place over boiling water; stir until sugar is completely dissolved (about 5 minutes). Remove from heat, but leave jelly over hot water. Stir in pectin at once. If foam forms on top, skim it off with a metal spoon. Proceed following step 6 on page 27. Makes 4 half pints.

Pickling Like a Pro

Whether you're an experienced hand at making pickles or just considering putting up your first batch, you'll get great satisfaction from our easy pickle-making procedures in this section. It includes a quick dill, a variety of sweet pickles, as well as pickled vegetables, fruits, relishes, and chutneys. None of the recipes requires the weeks of fermenting that sour pickles usually need.

Pickling generally applies to any food preserved in a brine or vinegar. This includes vegetables, fruits, relishes, and chutneys.

Pickles usually refer to cucumbers that have been preserved in a brine or vinegar. (To make old-fashioned pickles, see the special feature on page 37.)

Relishes may be automatically associated in most people's minds with hot dogs and hamburgers, but actually they have a much wider gastronomic potential. Piquant blends of vegetables, fruits, spices, and vinegar, they are a tasty accompaniment to any number of meats.

Chutneys are usually associated with Middle Eastern or Indian food, but they can be served as a condiment complementing a wide range of foods. They, too, are a type of relish, varying from hot and spicy to mild and tangy.

Use the right equipment

Make sure you have a kettle large enough to hold all your ingredients so they won't boil over the top as they cook. All utensils should be aluminum, stainless steel, enamelware, or glass. Copper may turn pickles an unappetizing shade of off-green, and iron turns them black. (Caution: the action of acid or salt with galvanized utensils can develop a poisonous substance.)

Use regular canning jars that are free from nicks and sharp edges. Rusty ring bands should be discarded.

Important ingredients

Fruits and vegetables should be firm, fresh, free of blemishes, and well washed. Preserve them as soon as possible after picking. Small to medium cucumbers may be left whole; any larger cucumbers should be sliced or cut into chunks. A regular cucumber has fewer spines than the pickling cucumber, is darker in color, and larger.

Pure granulated salt is preferable to table salt, which can be used but contains chemicals that could cause clouding or darkening of the pickles.

Vinegar should be a good, clear, standard one, free of sediment, with 4 to 5 percent acetic acid. Do not use a homemade one, for it may not be acetic enough. Distilled white vinegar best preserves the color in foods. Cider vinegar may cause darkening of the food but may be preferred for its flavor and aroma. (Avoid long boiling of vinegar, for boiling depletes the acetic acid, which is important in the preservation of pickles.)

Edible lactic acid may be substituted for some or all of the vinegar in recipes. It is available in a concentration of 50 percent acid. Since most vinegar is 5 percent acid, only 1/10 as much lactic acid is needed.

For best flavor, use fresh *spices*, such as dill and garlic.

Use *granulated cane or beet sugar*. Brown sugar tends to darken the color and gives a stronger flavor.

Water with a high iron content may cause darkening. (Do not use *alum* because it is difficult to measure the tiny amount needed for pickles at home. Too much can soften the pickles, as well as cause digestive disturbances.)

Step-by-step canning for pickles, relishes, and chutney

Some pickles, relishes, and chutneys are preserved by putting boiling hot food into boiling hot, sterilized jars; others by putting boiling hot food into hot jars and then simmering them in a canning kettle for a specified length of time.

Processing without a canner

1) Get out canning jars, lids, and ring bands. Check jars for nicks and cracks (see illustration, page 9). Discard these and any rusted or bent ring bands. Place jars in boiling water for 15 minutes to sterilize. Scald jar lids in boiling water and keep very hot until time to use.

2) Heat food to boiling in a large kettle for the prescribed time in each recipe.

3) Fill one hot jar at a time to the top with boiling hot food or to within head space called for in each recipe. Wipe each jar rim clean with a damp cloth.

4) Seal each jar as filled, with a lid and ring band, screwing down the band just as tight as is comfortable.

5) Let jars cool out of a draft on a folded towel. Leave on ring bands until the jars are cool to the touch.

6) Test for a good seal by pressing the lid with your finger. If it stays down when pressed, the jar is sealed. If any lid pops back up when pressed, the jar is not sealed. Store any unsealed jars in the refrigerator and use immediately. Store sealed jars in a cool, dry place. Refrigerate after opening.

Processing with a canner

1) Get out a canning kettle, jars, lids, ring bands, and any other accessories you might need (see page 7). Check jars for nicks and cracks (see illustration on page 9). Discard these and any rusted or bent ring bands. Canning jars and ring bands should be clean and hot (a dishwasher is ideal for both washing and keeping them hot). If you don't have a dishwasher, wash jars and then fill with hot water until used. Scald lids in boiling water and keep very hot until ready to use.

2) In a large kettle, heat food to boiling for the prescribed time in each recipe.

3) Place the rack in the canning kettle and fill the kettle about half full with hot water. Place the kettle, covered, on the range to heat. In a large teakettle or other pan, heat additional water to add later.

4) Fill hot pint-sized or half-pint-sized jars with boiling hot food to within ¼ inch of jar rim (quart jars to within ½ inch of rim) unless stated otherwise in the recipe.

5) Run a spatula down in between food and jar to release air bubbles. Fill with more cooking liquid, if necessary.

6) With a damp cloth, wipe off any spilled food from rim of jar and place lids on to seal. Screw on ring bands as tightly as you comfortably can.

7) Put jars on rack in canning kettle, making sure they don't touch the canner sides or each other. The hot water in the canner must cover jar lids by 1 to 2 inches (see illustration on page 10). Bring to simmering and keep water simmering throughout the processing time specified in each recipe (processing time is determined from the time the water begins to break).

8) Take jars out of water at end of processing time with a jar lifter, being careful not to disturb the lid seal (see illustration on page 10). Leave on ring bands until jars are cool.

9) Cool on a folded towel away from drafts. Check for a good seal by pressing lid with your finger. If it stays down when pressed, the jar is sealed. If it pops back up when pressed, it is not sealed. Store in a cool, dry area. Put any unsealed jars in the refrigerator and use quickly. Refrigerate all jars after opening.

Pickling Recipes

Quick Dill Pickles

4 pounds or 2 quarts cucumbers
6 teaspoons salt
3 cups each vinegar and water
9 heads fresh dill or 3 tablespoons
    dill seed
1 tablespoon whole mixed pickling spices
    (optional)
18 whole black peppers

Prepare 6 pint-sized or 3 quart-sized canning jars, following step 1 under *Processing with a canner* on page 31.

Wash the cucumbers thoroughly. If using larger than 4-inch cucumbers, slice, quarter, or halve lengthwise. In a large kettle or saucepan, combine salt, vinegar, and water. Bring to a boil.

Pack cucumbers into clean, hot jars. For each quart-sized jar, add 3 heads dill or 1 tablespoon dill seeds, 1 teaspoon pickling spices, and 6 whole black peppers.

Fill with boiling vinegar-salt solution to ½ inch from top of quart-sized jars or ¼ inch from top of pint-sized jars. Proceed with steps 3–9 under *Processing with a canner* on page 31. Process large (about 4-inch size) whole cucumbers for 10 minutes in pint-sized jars (20 minutes in quarts). Process smaller whole cucumbers, as well as slices, halves, or quarters, for 5 minutes in pint-sized jars (7 minutes in quarts). Makes 6 pints.

For kosher-style dill pickles, follow the recipe above, adding 2 cloves of garlic (peeled and halved) to each jar.

Mixed Sweet Cucumber Pickles

Soaking sliced cucumbers and vegetables in a salt-water solution helps to keep these spicy-sweet pickles crisp and crunchy. The recipe is a variation of one known as bread-and-butter pickles.

Cut 10 pounds unpeeled cucumbers (each about 1 to 1½ inches in diameter) into slices about ¼ inch thick.

Also cut 4 large green or red bell peppers (stem and seeds removed) and 4 pounds onions into 1-inch squares. Combine the 3 vegetables and sprinkle with ½ cup salt; cover with ice cold water and stir to blend. Let stand 3 hours, stirring often. Drain thoroughly.

Prepare 7 or 8 quart-sized canning jars and lids, following step 1 under *Processing without a canner* on page 31.

In a large kettle (8 qts. or larger), combine 5 cups *each* white wine vinegar and sugar, 1 cup water, 2 tablespoons *each* mustard and celery seed, 1 teaspoon turmeric, and ½ teaspoon ground cloves. Stir to dissolve sugar; then cover and bring to boiling. Add about half the drained vegetables and bring back to simmering, stirring. Simmer, uncovered, stirring for 3 to 5 minutes.

With a slotted spoon, ladle the vegetables into clean, hot canning jars, packing vegetables firmly so jars are well filled. Fill each jar to within ⅛ inch of the rim with pickling liquid. Reheat pickling liquid to boiling and add remaining vegetables; simmer as above.

Proceed with steps 3–6 under *Processing without a canner* on page 31. Makes 7 to 8 quarts.

Fresh Refrigerator Pickles

Refrigerator pickles require no canning. These paper-thin, mildly sweet, "fresh" pickles stay very crunchy up to about three weeks in the refrigerator. Serve them as a relish to go with meats.

Cut 2 unpeeled English or Armenian cucumbers or 3 large regular cucumbers (each about 1 to 1½ inches in diameter) into slices about 1/16 inch thick. Also finely chop 1 medium-sized green pepper (stem and seeds removed) and 1 medium-sized onion. Combine vegetables in a jar (about 1½-qt. size) or bowl and sprinkle with 1 tablespoon salt and 2 teaspoons celery seed. Stir gently and let stand for about 1 hour.

Combine ¾ cup sugar and ½ cup white vinegar and stir to dissolve sugar. Pour over vegetables and stir to blend. Cover and refrigerate.

Pickles are ready to eat in about a day; store, covered, in refrigerator. Makes about 5 cups.

Sweet Spiced Pickles

Similar to pickled watermelon rind, these spiced cucumber pickles are a good condiment to serve with meats. What makes them extra crisp is a powder called calcium hydroxide that is readily available from a building supply store.

About 10 pounds regular green
   cucumbers
1 bottle (0.4 oz.) calcium hydroxide
   (Powder #40)
4 quarts cold water
1 quart white vinegar
11 cups sugar
1 teaspoon each celery seed and whole
   cloves
1 teaspoon each salt and mixed pickling
   spice

Peel cucumbers and cut lengthwise into quarters. Scoop out and discard seeds and soft pulp. Cut into chunks 1½ inches long; you should have 5 quarts.

Stir together the calcium hydroxide and water until dissolved. Pour over cucumber pieces and let stand, uncovered, overnight; stir frequently.

Drain cucumbers and rinse well with large amounts of cold water. In a large kettle (at least 8 qts.), combine the vinegar and sugar. Add celery seed, cloves, salt, and pickling spice. Boil, stirring, for 5 minutes.

Add the drained cucumbers and bring back to boiling. Reduce heat and simmer, stirring often, until cucumbers are translucent (45 to 60 minutes).

Meanwhile, prepare 7 pint-sized canning jars, following step 1 under *Processing without a canner* on page 31. You can start filling the canning jars as soon as about half the cucumbers are translucent, picking out the clear pieces, ladling them into clean hot jars, and then filling them with syrup to within ¼ inch of the rim. Proceed with steps 3-6. Makes about 7 pints.

Armenian Pickled Mixed Vegetables

In markets that carry Middle Eastern foods you may have discovered the jars of pickled vegetables called *tourshee*. Armenians serve them as appetizers with cracker bread and cheese.

You can make them in a 2-gallon crock if you like or 3 half-gallon jars. Layer vegetables and seasonings in the crock, then set a plate with a weight on top to keep vegetables submerged in the brine; cover crock. They are ready to eat in a week or so. No canning is necessary.

3 cloves garlic, peeled crushed whole
1 to 3 small, dried, hot chile peppers
1 bunch (about 1 lb.) carrots, peeled and cut
   into 2-inch pieces (cut large carrots
   lengthwise in halves)
6 large stalks celery (coarse strings
   removed), cut into 2-inch pieces
1 head cauliflower (about 1 lb.), broken
   into flowerets
1 head cabbage (about 2 lbs.), cut into 12
   wedges
2 green or red bell peppers, seeded and
   cut into 1½-inch squares
2 large, sweet onions cut in 1-inch squares
3 teaspoons mixed pickling spices
3⅓ cups cider vinegar
10 cups water
5 tablespoons salt

Drop 1 clove garlic into each of 3 half-gallon jars or into a 2-gallon crock. Put ⅓ to 1 chile pepper into each jar, washing your hands immediately after handling them as these peppers can burn. Distribute the carrots, celery, cauliflower, cabbage, red or green peppers, and onion equally between the jars.

Spoon 1 teaspoon mixed pickling spices into each of the jars. Then in a saucepan, heat the cider vinegar with the water and salt to boiling; pour over vegetables. Put lids on jars or weight on crock and store in the refrigerator or in a cool place, such as garage or unheated room, for at least a week. Chill before serving. Makes 6 quarts.

Giardiniera (Pickled Vegetables)

The brightly colored, pickled mixed vegetables you see in fancy food stores and Italian delicatessens can be made at home. Called *giardiniera*, they can be served as appetizers or with meats.

2 or 3 bunches small carrots (about ¾
   inch wide at top)
1 small bunch celery
2 red bell or green peppers
1 large (about 2 lbs.) cauliflower
1 pound pickling or small, white boiling
   onions
1 cup salt
4 quarts cold water
2 quarts white vinegar
¼ cup mustard seed
2 tablespoons celery seed
1 small dried hot chile pepper
2½ cups sugar

(Continued on next page)

Peel carrots and cut in half lengthwise and then in 1½-inch-long pieces—enough to measure 4 cups. Remove strings from celery, slice lengthwise, and cut into 1½-inch-long pieces; measure 3 cups. Remove seeds and stems from peppers and cut into 1-inch-wide strips. Break cauliflower into 1½-inch-thick flowerets and trim stems. Peel onions. Combine vegetables in a bowl with the salt dissolved in the water. Let stand, covered, in the refrigerator 12 to 18 hours (overnight); then drain, rinse in cold water, and drain again.

For pickling, combine the vinegar, mustard seed, celery seed, chile pepper, and sugar in a 6-quart stainless steel or enamel pan; bring to boiling and boil for 3 minutes. Add vegetables and boil 10 minutes or until vegetables are almost tender. Discard chile.

To can, prepare 6 pint-sized canning jars, following step 1 under *Processing without a canner* on page 31. Proceed with steps 3–6. Makes 6 pints.

Pickled Artichokes

When artichokes are plentiful in the markets, you might consider pickling the smaller ones (sometimes called *hearts*).

You pickle them, and then let them stand a month before using. Serve as they are or marinate. To marinate, drain and mix artichokes with an oil (preferably olive oil) and vinegar dressing; then sprinkle with freshly minced parsley.

> **About 6½ dozen artichokes, each about 2 by 3 inches (not measuring stem)**
> **Acidified water (see below)**
> **3 quarts water**
> **3 cups white wine vinegar (5 percent acidity)**
> **4½ teaspoons salt**
> **6 medium-sized or 12 small dried hot chile peppers**
> **6 medium-sized or 12 small cloves garlic**
> **About ¾ cup minced parsley (optional)**

Trim artichokes by cutting off the stem and top ⅓ of each artichoke. Then break off all the coarse bracts clear down to the very tender yellowish inner bracts. Trim stem end to make cone shape without cutting away any more of the bottom than necessary. Drop immediately into enough *acidified water* to cover (½ cup vinegar to each quart of water). Keep artichokes immersed as much as possible by floating a pan lid or inverted plastic plate on the water (even though some darken, they will lighten when cooked).

When all artichokes are trimmed, combine the

3 quarts water, wine vinegar, and salt in a large pan (not cast iron, it blackens artichokes) and bring to a boil. Add artichokes (drained of acidified water) and return to boil; then simmer until barely tender (about 10 minutes).

Meanwhile, prepare 6 pint-sized or 12 half-pint-sized wide-mouth canning jars, following step 1 found under *Processing without a canner* on page 31.

With a slotted spoon, lift hot artichokes from water and arrange in hot, sterilized jars; a pint will hold 12 to 13 artichokes, a half pint 6 or 7. To each pint, add 1 medium-sized chile pepper, 1 medium-sized clove garlic, and 2 tablespoons parsley (if you wish). To each half pint, add a small chile, small clove garlic, and 1 tablespoon parsley. Bring cooking water to a boil and pour into jars to cover artichokes; there should be about ¼ inch space to the rim of each jar. Proceed with steps 3–6 under *Processing without a canner* on page 31. Store in a cool, dark place for a month before using. Makes 6 pints or 12 half pints.

Pickled Onions, English Style

The English serve these whole, small pickled onions as appetizers. The tart marinade cuts the heat of the raw onions and adds a spicy, piquant flavor.

If the boiling onions you find in your market are larger than about ¾ inch in diameter, pickle them whole; then cut in quarters to serve.

You can keep the pickled onions in the refrigerator for up to a month.

> **½ cup salt**
> **3 cups cold water**
> **2 pounds small white boiling onions, peeled**
> **2 cups (1 pint) white vinegar**
> **¼ cup firmly packed dark brown sugar**
> **1 teaspoon each whole allspice, mustard seed, whole black peppers, and mixed pickling spice**

In a large bowl, stir the salt with water until dissolved; then add onions. Cover and refrigerate for 12 to 24 hours.

Drain onions, cover with cold water, drain again, and pack in a crock having 1½ quart capacity or 3 pint-sized canning jars (see below). In a saucepan, stir together the vinegar, brown sugar, allspice, mustard seed, whole peppers, and pickling spice; bring to boiling. Pour hot marinade over onions. Let cool, cover, and refrigerate for at least a week before serving. Makes 3 pints or 1½ quarts.

To can, prepare 3 pint-sized wide-mouth, canning jars following step 1 under *Processing with a canner* on page 31. Then proceed with steps 3–9. Process 10 minutes. Makes 3 pints.

Spiced Pickled Quince

When ripe in late September and October, the quince is most commonly used to make jelly. Yet this generally neglected fruit also makes a delicious condiment to serve with meats when sliced and cooked in a spiced sugar syrup. Pack in jars, and enjoy now or store for Christmas giving.

    8 to 10 large quince
2½ cups boiling water
 16 whole cloves
    2 large whole oranges, cut in ¼-inch slices
    6 cups sugar
    2 cups white vinegar
    1 stick (about 3 inches) cinnamon

Peel, core, and cut fruit into ¾-inch wedges (you should have 12 cups). In a large pan, cook in the boiling water until just tender when pierced (about 5 minutes) stirring gently several times so the fruit cooks evenly. Drain, reserving 1½ cups liquid.

In the same pan, combine the reserved 1½ cups liquid, cloves, orange slices, sugar, vinegar, and cinnamon. Bring to a boil and boil gently, uncovered, for 10 minutes. Add quince and boil for 30 minutes longer, stirring occasionally.

Meanwhile, prepare 6 pint-sized canning jars, following step 1 under *Processing without a canner* on page 31. Proceed with steps 3-6. Makes 6 pints.

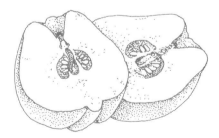

Spicy Pickled Figs

Mild, sweet Mission figs have a most accommodating nature for pickling. The heat of this pickling process develops their sweetness and helps them absorb the spicy flavor of the vinegar bath

in which they cook. And the blue-black figs turn to a rich shade of burgundy.

The flavor is both tart and sweet, with hints of cinnamon and clove. These canned pickled figs make a good relish to accompany steaks and chops.

    4 pounds firm ripe Mission (Black Mission) figs
2½ cups sugar
1½ cups white vinegar
    2 sticks cinnamon (each about 1½ inches long)
    1 tablespoon whole cloves

Gently wash figs, leaving stems intact. In a 6-quart saucepan, combine the sugar, vinegar, cinnamon sticks, and cloves; over medium heat, bring to boiling, stirring. Boil until liquid is reduced to 1½ cups (about 15 minutes). Add figs, cover, and simmer figs about 15 minutes (figs should still hold their shape). Shake pan occasionally; avoid stirring, because it breaks up fruit.

Meanwhile, prepare 4 pint-sized canning jars, following step 1 under *Processing without a canner* on page 31. With slotted spoon, lift figs from boiling syrup and pack into jar; then ladle boiling syrup into jar to within ½-inch of rim. Proceed with steps 3-6. Makes 4 pints.

Spiced Apple Rings

    6 cups sugar
1⅔ cups cider vinegar
    1 teaspoon red food coloring
    4 sticks whole cinnamon (each about 2 inches long)
    2 teaspoons whole cloves
       About 4 pounds firm-ripe Golden Delicious apples, peeled and cored

Prepare 4 pint-sized canning jars, following step 1 under *Processing without a canner* on page 31.

In a 5-quart or larger pan, combine sugar, vinegar, food coloring, cinnamon, and cloves. Bring to a boil and simmer, uncovered, for 10 minutes.

Slice the apples crosswise into about ⅓-inch-thick rings. Add about half of the rings to the simmering syrup and cook, turning rings occasionally, until apples are barely tender when pierced and just beginning to turn translucent around the edges (6 to 8 minutes). Proceed with steps 3-6 under *Processing without a canner*, filling 2 of the jars to within ½ inch of rim. Then simmer remaining apples; fill and can remaining 2 jars as above. Let stand at least 1 week before using. Makes 4 pints.

Spiced Pickled Seckel Pears

Their small size—about 2 inches in diameter—makes the Seckel pear variety an ideal choice to preserve whole. Here the pears, pickled and spiced with cinnamon and cloves, make a dramatic relish for meats.

- **1 cup white vinegar**
- **3½ cups sugar**
- **¾ teaspoon ground cloves**
- **¼ teaspoon ground allspice**
- **4 sticks whole cinnamon (each about 2 inches long)**
- **4 pounds firm-ripe Seckel pears**

In a 6-quart saucepan, combine the vinegar, sugar, cloves, allspice, and cinnamon; set aside.

Wash pears gently, leaving stems intact if possible. With a vegetable peeler, cut peel from pears. Bring vinegar mixture to boiling; add pears, cover, and simmer gently until pears are tender but not soft (about 20 minutes).

Meanwhile, prepare 2 quart-sized canning jars, following step 1 under *Processing without a canner* on page 31. Proceed with steps 3-6. Makes 2 quarts.

Dutch Beets

- **2 tablespoons butter or margarine**
- **1 tablespoon all-purpose flour**
- **¾ cup boiling water**
- **1 tablespoon sugar**
- **¼ teaspoon salt**
- **1 cup vinegar**
- **2 teaspoons minced onion**
- **Dash of pepper**
- **2 cups sliced or diced cooked beets**

In a saucepan, melt butter and stir in flour; add boiling water and cook, stirring constantly, until mixture is thick and smooth. Add sugar, salt, vinegar, onion, pepper, and beets; heat slowly for 10 to 15 minutes. Serves 4.

To can, follow steps 1-9 under *Processing with a canner* on page 31. Process pints 35 minutes. Makes 1 pint.

Pumpkin Pickles

In a 5-quart pan, combine 2¼ cups sugar with 2¼ cups cider vinegar and 3 cups water. Add 3 sticks cinnamon (*each* about 2 inches long) and 15 whole cloves. Bring to a boil and boil gently for 10 minutes. Meanwhile, cut a 4-pound pumpkin into sections. Scrape out the pulp and seeds and cut off rind; cut pumpkin meat into 1-inch squares (you should have 6 cups); add to syrup.

Boil gently for 5 minutes. Remove from heat, cover, and allow to stand for 1 hour. Return to heat and boil gently, uncovered, until pieces are translucent (about 60 minutes) turning pieces occasionally. Store in refrigerator.

To can, prepare 5 half-pint-sized canning jars, following step 1 under *Processing with a canner* on page 31. Continue with steps 3–9, packing boiling hot pickles into jars. Process for 10 minutes. Makes 5 half pints.

Red Cabbage

- **1 tablespoon butter or margarine**
- **1 medium-sized head red cabbage, shredded**
- **1 tart apple, peeled, cored, and diced**
- **1¼ cup dry red wine**
- **1 teaspoon salt**
- **4 tablespoons red wine vinegar**
- **4 tablespoons firmly packed brown sugar**
- **2 whole cloves**
- **Apple slices for garnish**

Melt butter or margarine in a heavy pan. Add shredded cabbage, diced apple, ¼ cup of the wine, and the salt. Cover and cook, stirring occasionally, until cabbage is just limp (about 5 minutes). Add 1 cup more wine, the vinegar, brown sugar, and cloves. Simmer, covered, for about 1½ hours; stir occasionally. Add more wine if needed. Discard cloves. Garnish with apple-slices when ready to serve. Makes 4 to 6 servings.

To can, follow steps 1-9 for *Processing with a canner* on page 31. Process for 20 minutes. Makes 1 quart.

Easy Pickles

If you have a fondness for the taste of homemade pickles but don't like to can, these three easy pickle recipes will seem made to order.

Sweet Freezer Chips

To make sweet freezer chips, you simply layer sliced cucumbers and onions in freezer jars or containers and freeze them in a vinegar and sugar syrup. To serve, just thaw what you need.

    2½ pounds (about 5 medium-size)
          cucumbers
      1 medium-size mild white onion
      2 tablespoons salt
      2 quarts ice cubes
      4 cups sugar
      2 cups cider vinegar

Cut unpeeled cucumbers in ⅛-inch-thick slices; you should have 2 quarts. Thinly slice onion. Mix cucumber and onion slices with salt in large bowl; cover mixture with ice cubes and refrigerate for 2 to 3 hours.

Drain off water and discard unmelted ice cubes; do not rinse. Pack cucumber and onion slices in freezer containers or canning jars to within 1½ inches from top.

In a 2-quart pan, combine sugar and vinegar and bring to a boil, stirring, until sugar dissolves. Pour just enough hot syrup over cucumbers to cover. Place on lids. Cool, then freeze at least one week.

To serve, place container to thaw in the refrigerator at least 8 hours. Makes about 3 pints.

Spicy Seven-day Pickles

It takes just seven days until these pickles are ready to serve. They have a sweet taste similar to pickled watermelon rind.

    3½ pounds (about 8 medium-size)
          cucumbers
      4 cups sugar
      2 cups white vinegar
      1 tablespoon whole mixed pickling
          spice
      2 teaspoons salt

Scrub whole unpeeled cucumbers, place in a deep bowl, and cover with boiling water. Let stand overnight. The next day, drain cucumbers, cover again with boiling water, and let stand overnight. Repeat the process on the third and fourth days. On the fifth day, cut cucumbers in ¼-inch-thick slices and return them to the clean deep bowl.

In a 3-quart pan combine sugar, vinegar, pickling spice, and salt. Bring to a boil to dissolve sugar; pour over cucumbers. Cool, then cover bowl and refrigerate two days.

On the seventh day bring cucumbers and syrup just to a boil, then pack into hot clean jars; place on lids. Allow to cool, then store in the refrigerator. Will keep up to three months. Makes about 5 pints.

Bread and Butter Slices

These refrigerator pickles are less sweet than the seven-day variety. The pickles cook briefly in a spicy mustard syrup before they are packed into jars.

    3½ pounds (about 8 medium-size)
          cucumbers
    2½ cups sugar
      2 cups cider vinegar
      1 cup water
      1 teaspoon each salt and celery seed
      1 tablespoon whole mustard seed
    1½ tablespoons whole mixed pickling
          spice

Cut unpeeled cucumbers in ¼-inch slices; set aside.

In a 5-quart (or larger) pan, combine sugar, vinegar, water, salt, celery seed, mustard seed, and pickling spice. Bring to a boil, stirring to dissolve sugar. Add cucumber slices to syrup and return mixture to a boil, turning cucumbers gently with a wooden spoon to coat with syrup. Continue boiling 1½ minutes; remove from heat.

Ladle hot cucumber slices and pickling liquid into hot clean jars; place on lids. Cool, then refrigerate. Will keep in refrigerator for up to 3 months. Makes about 5 pints.

Relish Recipes

Tomato Relish

Long, slow cooking concentrates the spicy ginger flavor of this relish.

- **8 pounds tomatoes (about 16)**
  Boiling water
- **3 large onions, chopped**
- **5 large green apples, peeled, cored, and sliced**
- **3 whole lemons, thinly sliced**
- **4 tablespoons (about 6 oz.) grated fresh ginger root**
- **3 cloves garlic, minced or mashed**
- **½ cup sugar**
- **1 tablespoon salt**
- **2 tablespoons mustard seed**
- **1 teaspoon ground cloves**
- **¼ teaspoon cayenne**
- **1½ cups each white wine vinegar and honey**

Dip tomatoes in boiling water for about 20 seconds. Rinse in cold water, peel, and cut out stem.

In a kettle (about 12-qt. size), combine tomatoes, onions, apples, lemons, ginger, garlic, sugar, salt, mustard seed, cloves, cayenne, vinegar, and honey; bring to boiling. Reduce heat and simmer gently, uncovered, for about 6 hours or until reduced to about 7 pints; stir often during last hour.

Meanwhile, prepare 7 pint-sized canning jars, following step 1 under *Processing with a canner* on page 31. Then proceed with steps 3-9. Process 15 minutes. Makes 7 pints.

Tomato-Apple Relish

This tomato-apple relish is sweet and particularly good spooned over grilled hamburgers and sausages.

Peel and chop enough ripe tomatoes to measure 6 cups (about 4 lbs.). Also peel and chop enough tart apples to measure 4 cups (takes about 3 large apples).

In a 4 to 5-quart kettle, combine the tomatoes and apples with 4 cups finely chopped onion (about 3 large), 2 *each* red and green bell peppers (finely chopped), 1 cup raisins, 1 teaspoon salt, ¾ cup firmly packed brown sugar, 1 cup cider vinegar, 1 tablespoon mustard seed, 1½ teaspoons celery seed, and 1 teaspoon ground turmeric. Bring the mixture to a boil over high heat. Reduce heat to medium-low and cook, stirring frequently to prevent sticking, for 1 hour or until mixture is quite thick and all liquid has been absorbed.

Meanwhile, prepare 4 pint-sized canning jars, following step 1 under *Processing with a canner* on page 31. Then proceed with steps 3-9. Process for 10 minutes. Makes 4 pints.

Zucchini Relish

This colorful zucchini relish is crisp and tart. It goes well with anything.

- **5 pounds zucchini (about 20 medium-sized)**
- **6 large onions**
- **½ cup salt**
  Cold water
- **2 cups white wine vinegar**
- **1 cup sugar**
- **1 teaspoon dry mustard**
- **2 teaspoons celery seed**
- **½ teaspoon each ground cinnamon and nutmeg, and pepper**
- **2 jars (4 oz. each) pimientos, chopped**

Put zucchini and onions through a food chopper, using a medium blade, or chop; mix with salt in a bowl and cover with water. Cover and refrigerate for 4 hours or overnight.

Drain vegetables, rinse; then drain again. In a 5 or 6-quart pan, combine vegetables, vinegar, sugar, dry mustard, celery seed, cinnamon, nutmeg, pepper, and pimientos. Bring quickly to boiling, stirring constantly. Reduce heat and simmer, uncovered, for about 20 minutes or until reduced to about 3 quarts (or 6 pints).

Prepare 6 pint-sized canning jars, following step 1 under *Processing with a canner* on page 31. Then proceed with steps 3-9. Process for 15 minutes. Makes 6 pints.

Cucumber Relish

You'll enjoy this relish on frankfurters.

12 large cucumbers, peeled
 4 large onions
 6 green peppers, stems and seeds removed
 4 teaspoons each celery seed and mustard seed
 1 teaspoon salt
 ½ teaspoon ground cloves
 1 tablespoon ground turmeric
3½ cups cider vinegar
2½ cups sugar

Put the cucumbers, onions, and green peppers through a food chopper, using a medium blade, or chop. In a 5 or 6-quart saucepan, combine vegetables, celery seed, mustard seed, salt, cloves, turmeric, vinegar, and sugar. Quickly bring to boiling, stirring constantly; reduce heat and simmer for about 3 hours or until reduced to about 5 pints.

Prepare 5 pint-sized canning jars, following step 1 under *Processing with a canner* on page 31. Then proceed with steps 3-9. Process for 15 minutes. Makes 5 pints.

Spicy Tomato Catsup

Making homemade catsup is an easy way to use an over-abundance of tomatoes. A blender helps speed the process.

12 pounds fully ripe tomatoes, coarsely chopped
 2 large onions, cut into pieces
 1 red bell pepper, seeded and cut into pieces
 1 tablespoon each mustard seed, whole black peppers, and basil leaves
 2 teaspoons whole allspice
 2 small dried hot chile peppers
 1 large bay leaf
 1 stick cinnamon (about 3 inches long)
1½ cups firmly packed brown sugar
 1 tablespoon each salt and paprika
 1 cup vinegar

In a covered blender jar, whirl tomatoes, onions, and peppers, a small amount at a time, until smooth. Press through a wire strainer and discard pulp. You should have 6 quarts of purée.

In at least an 8-quart kettle, bring purée to boiling over medium-high heat. Boil gently, uncovered, until reduced by about half; this takes about 1 hour. Stir often.

Put the mustard seed, black pepper, basil, all-spice, hot chile peppers, bay leaf, and cinnamon stick into a loosely tied cheesecloth bag. Add to purée. Then add the brown sugar, salt, and paprika. Continue cooking over medium to medium-high heat until very thick (about 1½ to 2 hours). As mixture thickens, stir often and reduce heat to prevent sticking. Add the vinegar during the last 10 to 15 minutes of cooking. Discard spice bag.

You can chill the catsup, pour into freezer containers, cover, and freeze, if you like; or it may be canned.

To can, prepare 4 pint-sized canning jars, following step 1 on page 9. Fill jars to within ¼ inch of rim. Then proceed with steps 3 and 5-9, processing for 20 minutes. Makes 2 quarts.

Hot and Spicy Chile Sauce

Serve this sauce spooned onto hot dogs, hamburgers, or steaks.

4 to 5 pounds fully ripe tomatoes
 1 large onion, chopped
 ¾ cup sugar
1¼ cups cider vinegar
 1 teaspoon crushed red pepper (seeds removed)
 1 teaspoon each mustard seed and salt
 ½ teaspoon each ground ginger and nutmeg
 ¼ teaspoon curry powder

Peel, core, and coarsely chop the tomatoes (you should have 8 cups). In a 5-quart Dutch oven, combine the tomatoes, onion, sugar, vinegar, red pepper, mustard seed, salt, ginger, nutmeg, and curry powder. Bring to boiling; then reduce heat and simmer gently until reduced to about 2 pints; it takes about 2 hours. As mixture thickens, stir frequently to prevent sticking.

Meanwhile, prepare 2 pint-sized canning jars, following step 1 on page 9. Then proceed, following steps 3 and 5-9, filling jars to within ⅛ inch of rim. Process 15 minutes. Makes 2 pints.

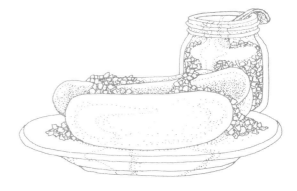

Seasoned Tomato Paste

Making your own tomato paste is an economical way to "put up" tomatoes. Incorporate the seasoned paste into recipes calling for canned tomato paste.

    15 pounds fully ripe tomatoes, coarsely
        chopped (you should have about 8
        quarts)
     4 large red or green bell peppers, seeded
        and coarsely chopped
     3 medium-sized onions, coarsely chopped
     4 medium-sized carrots, coarsely chopped
     2 or 3 cloves garlic, coarsely chopped

Whirl in a blender the tomatoes, peppers, onions, carrots, and garlic, a small amount at a time, until smooth. Press through a wire strainer and discard pulp.

In a 12-quart kettle, bring purée to boiling over medium-high heat. Boil gently, uncovered, until thick enough to mound on a spoon (about 5 hours). As mixture thickens, stir often, reduce heat, and partially cover.

Chill, pour into freezer containers, cover, and freeze or can as directed below.

To can, prepare 5 pint-sized canning jars, following step 1 on page 9. Fill jars to within ¼ inch of rim. Then proceed with step 3 and 5-9, processing for 30 minutes. Makes 5 pints.

Cranberry Relish

Deep red cranberry relish shows off handsomely in jars and makes a tasty condiment to serve with the traditional holiday turkey or other meats.

     1 pound (4 cups) cranberries
     1 medium-sized orange
     1 cup raisins
     1 medium-sized onion, chopped
     ½ cup chopped green pepper
     1 clove garlic, minced or mashed
     2 tablespoons minced fresh ginger
     1 cup cider vinegar
     1 can (6 oz.) frozen cranberry juice
        concentrate
     2 cups sugar
     ½ teaspoon salt
     ¼ teaspoon each cayenne and ground
        cloves
     1 teaspoon mustard seed

Rinse cranberries, drain, and coarsely chop; put into a 5-quart pan. Cut thin outer peel off orange; cut peel into slivers and add to pan. Cut off all white membrane, hold orange over pan, and lift out sections; add to pan along with raisins, onion, green pepper, garlic, ginger, vinegar, and cranberry juice concentrate.

Bring to a boil, stirring occasionally; boil 10 minutes. Add sugar, salt, cayenne, cloves, and mustard seed. Boil gently, stirring more often as mixture thickens, for about 20 minutes. Store in refrigerator or can.

To can, prepare 5 half-pint-sized canning jars, following step 1 under *Processing with a canner* on page 31. Then proceed with steps 3-9, processing for 10 minutes. Makes 5 half pints.

Whole Cranberry Orange Sauce

Tart, whole-berry cranberry sauce, a traditional holiday relish, is easy to put up in jars. In this recipe, the berries are accented with orange juice and sweetened with brown sugar.

     4 cups (1 lb.) fresh cranberries
     2 cups firmly packed brown sugar
     3 tablespoons frozen orange juice
        concentrate, undiluted
    1¼ cups water

Wash and drain the cranberries. In a 3-quart or larger pan, combine the berries, sugar, orange juice, and water. Bring to boiling and boil, uncovered, until most of the berries open (about 5 minutes).

To can, prepare 2 pint-sized canning jars, following step 1 under *Processing with a canner* on page 31. Then proceed with steps 3-9. Process 15 minutes for pints, 20 minutes for quarts. Makes 2 pints.

Cranberry Applesauce. Stir together 2 cups applesauce (see directions on the fruit canning chart under *Purées* on page 13) with 2 cups Cranberry Orange Sauce (recipe above). Cover and chill before serving. Makes 6 servings.

To can, follow directions for canning Whole Cranberry Orange Sauce above, processing pints 15 minutes. Makes 2 pints.

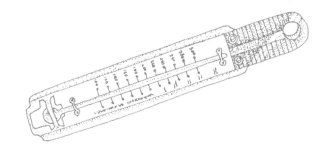

Chutney Recipes

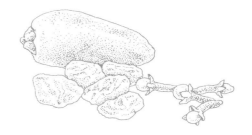

Papaya-Plum Chutney

1¼ cups cider vinegar
1¾ cups sugar
½ cup golden raisins
2 cloves garlic, minced or mashed
3 tablespoons chopped crystallized ginger
1 cinnamon stick (about 2 inches long)
1½ teaspoons salt
⅛ to ¼ teaspoon cayenne
2 large (about 1 lb. each) ripe papayas
2 pounds firm red plums

In a Dutch oven, combine the vinegar, sugar, raisins, garlic, ginger, cinnamon stick, salt, and cayenne. Bring to boiling; reduce heat and simmer, uncovered, for 1½ hours or until thickened. Stir often. Peel papayas, cut in halves, and discard seeds. Cut fruit into ½-inch squares. Quarter plums and discard pits. Add fruit to syrup and simmer until papaya is tender (about 30 minutes); stir occasionally. Discard cinnamon stick.

Meanwhile, prepare 3 pint-sized canning jars, following step 1 under *Processing with a canner* on page 31. Proceed with steps 3-9. Process for 5 minutes. Makes 3 pints.

Pineapple-Orange Chutney

3 large oranges
2 cups vinegar
1 cup firmly packed brown sugar
1 large onion, chopped
1 clove garlic, minced or mashed
1 teaspoon salt
½ teaspoon each ground cloves and
    allspice
⅛ to ¼ teaspoon cayenne
1 cinnamon stick (about 2 inches long)
1 cup chopped, pitted dates
½ cup raisins
1 large (about 4 lbs.) ripe pineapple

With a vegetable peeler, carefully remove the thin outer peel from 1 of the oranges; cut it into thin slivers and set aside. Holding the oranges over a bowl to catch their juices, cut the peel and white

membrane off all of the oranges; lift out sections and set aside.

In a Dutch oven, combine the vinegar, brown sugar, onion, garlic, salt, cloves, allspice, cayenne, cinnamon, dates, and raisins. Bring to a boil; reduce heat, add orange peel, and simmer 30 minutes or until slightly thickened.

Slice ends off pineapple; cut off rind deep enough to remove eyes. Slice pineapple lengthwise into quarters and slice off core, then cut into small cubes. Add pineapple to syrup and simmer, uncovered, 1½ hours or until mixture is quite thick. Stir in orange sections and not more than ¼ cup of the orange juice. Bring to simmering again.

To can, prepare 3 pint-sized canning jars, following step 1 under *Processing with a canner* on page 31. Proceed with steps 3-9. Process 5 minutes. Makes 3 pints.

Mango-Peach Chutney

Although mangoes make delicious traditional chutneys, they can be quite costly when used alone in the quantities needed for preparing chutney. One way to stretch their flavor is to combine them with peaches.

1½ cups each sugar and white vinegar
1 large onion, chopped
1 green pepper, seeded and diced
1 clove garlic, minced or mashed
1 lime, thinly sliced
1½ teaspoons ground cinnamon
½ teaspoon each ground cloves and
    allspice
1 teaspoon salt
⅛ to ¼ teaspoon cayenne
½ cup raisins
3 large (about 2½ lbs.) ripe mangoes
2 pounds peaches

In a Dutch oven, combine the sugar, vinegar, onion, green pepper, garlic, lime, cinnamon, cloves, allspice, salt, cayenne, and raisins. Bring to a boil; reduce heat and simmer, uncovered, for about 1 hour or until thickened. Stir the mixture frequently to prevent sticking.

Peel and slice the flesh from the seeds of the mangoes (you should have about 3½ cups fruit). Peel, pit, and slice the peaches. Add mangoes and peaches to the thickened syrup and simmer, uncovered, until fruit is tender (about 30 minutes); stir occasionally.

To can, prepare 3 pint-sized canning jars, following step 1 under *Processing with a canner* on page 31. Then proceed with steps 3-9, processing for 5 minutes. Makes 3 pints.

Plum-Nut Chutney

You add pecans to this dark, rich-tasting plum chutney when it is fully cooked.

1½ cups granulated sugar
1 cup cider vinegar
2 tablespoons minced fresh ginger (or 1½ teaspoons ground ginger)
1½ teaspoons ground mace
1 teaspoon salt
4 small dried hot chile peppers, crushed
1 small clove garlic, mashed
1 cup raisins or currants
4 pounds firm red plums, pitted, quartered
1 cup chopped pecans

Combine the sugar, vinegar, ginger, mace, salt, peppers, garlic, and raisins or currants in a large pan (4 qt.). Bring to a boil; then add the plums. Return to boiling and simmer about 30 minutes or until slightly thickened, stirring frequently to prevent sticking. Stir in the pecans.

To can, prepare 3 pint-sized canning jars, following step 2 under *Processing with a canner* on page 31. Proceed with steps 3-9, processing for 5 minutes. Makes 3 pints.

Apricot Chutney

You can buy the tamarind syrup used in this light-colored apricot chutney in Italian and specialty markets, but it's an optional addition here. The chutney is medium hot; for a milder version, omit the seeds from the peppers or use fewer peppers than the recipe designates.

1 cup each granulated sugar, firmly packed brown sugar, and cider vinegar
1 tablespoon finely chopped fresh ginger (or ¾ teaspoon ground ginger)
1 teaspoon ground allspice
1 teaspoon dry mustard
Dash ground cloves
3 small dried hot chile peppers, crushed
2 tablespoons tamarind syrup (optional)
1 small whole lime, chopped (about ½ cup)
½ cup chopped onion
1 small clove garlic, mashed
1 cup currants or raisins
4 pounds apricots, pitted and quartered (about 2½ qts.)

Combine the granulated and brown sugars, vinegar, ginger, allspice, mustard, cloves, peppers, tamarind syrup, lime, onion, garlic, and currants or raisins in a large pan (about 4 qt.-size). Bring to a boil; then add apricots. Return to boiling and simmer about 45 minutes or until slightly thickened, stirring frequently to prevent sticking.

Prepare 4 pint-sized canning jars, following step 1 under *Processing with a canner* on page 31. Then proceed with steps 3-9, processing 5 minutes. Makes 4 pints.

Rhubarb Chutney Sauce

8 cups coarsely chopped rhubarb (about 2½ lbs.)
1 cup each chopped onion and seedless raisins or currants
2 cups firmly packed brown sugar
½ cup cider vinegar
1 teaspoon salt
½ teaspoon each ground cinnamon, ginger, and allspice

Combine the rhubarb, onion, raisins or currants, sugar, vinegar, salt, cinnamon, ginger, and allspice. Bring to a full rolling boil; simmer over medium heat until thickened (about 25 minutes). Stir frequently.

To can, prepare 5 half-pint-sized canning jars, following step 2 under *Processing with a canner* on page 31. Then proceed with steps 3-9, processing 10 minutes. Makes 5 half pints.

Canning Fresh Vegetables

Before deciding to can vegetables, you should be aware that the only safe way to can them (as well as meats, poultry, or fish) is to process them under 10 pounds of pressure using a steam pressure canner. At these high temperatures, you'll have to expect some loss of flavor and some food value.

Never process vegetables in a regular canning kettle, using the boiling water method prescribed for canning fruits and tomatoes. Such heat treatment is not sufficient to prevent dangerous food spoilage in these low-acid foods. And never use the old-fashioned oven canning method for any produce. An oven provides a slow rate of heat transfer, as well as uneven heat distribution. Jars can explode.

Equipment you'll need

The only difference between the equipment needed for canning vegetables and that needed for fruits is that vegetables require a steam pressure canner. Otherwise, the equipment is the same.

The steam pressure canner is a heavy kettle with a tight-fitting cover that can be locked down to make it steam-tight. The cover is fitted with a safety valve, a petcock vent, and a pressure gauge.

There are two types of canners available; one has a weighted gauge and the other has a dial. The *weighted gauge* automatically limits pressure by a control pre-set for 5, 10, or 15 pounds. All our canning requires 10 pounds (240° F) pressure. The weighted control is simple, accurate, and never needs calibrating.

The *dial control* indicates the pressure on a numbered instrument and needs to be checked periodically for accuracy. Check it every season before using, following manufacturer's directions. The manufacturer will check it for you, as will county agricultural agents (or the Cooperative Extension Service) when they are equipped to do so. A new pressure gauge can be purchased for a few dollars. Whenever steam starts escaping from under the lid, it's time for a new neoprene gasket, which also costs only a few dollars.

It is safe to use your canner if the gauge registers on a pound or two high or low, but if it reads as much as 5 pounds off, replace the gauge. The following table tells how much to adjust your gauge if 1-4 pounds off.

If the gauge reads high—

    1 pound high—process at 11 pounds
    2 pounds high—process at 12 pounds
    3 pounds high—process at 13 pounds
    4 pounds high—process at 14 pounds

If the gauge reads low—

    1 pound low—process at 9 pounds
    2 pounds low—process at 8 pounds
    3 pounds low—process at 7 pounds
    4 pounds low—process at 6 pounds

The everyday "pressure cooker" pot designed for fast cooking should never be used for canning.

Use a rack in the bottom of the steam pressure canner with lots of openings so the steam can circulate. If it's a wire rack, make sure it's stable enough that jars won't tilt or touch the bottom of the canner. If using two layers of jars, make sure there is enough space above the lower jars to separate them.

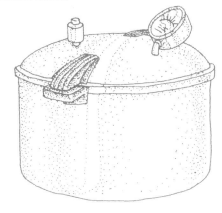

Other necessary equipment that you'll need includes jars, lids, ring bands, and the helpful accessories listed on page 7.

Step-by-step canning for vegetables

1) Get out the steam pressure canner (see under *Equipment you'll need* on page 43), canning jars, lids, ring bands, and the other helpful accessories listed on page 7. Check jars for nicks or cracks that might prevent a good seal. Discard these and any rusted or bent ring bands (see illustration on page 9). Canning jars and ring bands need to be clean. Scald lids just before using. You'll also need a large cooking pot for precooking the vegetables.

2) Place the rack in the pressure canner and fill the bottom with 2 to 3 inches of hot water (enough to keep it from boiling dry). The water can come to within 2-3 inches of the jar tops. With smaller jars, use a rack that is high enough to allow at least 2 inches of water in the canner bottom. Cover canner to bring water to a boil faster and keep it hot while preparing the vegetables.

3) Use fresh, firm, crisp vegetables, preparing only enough to fill one canner load at a time.

Prepare one load at a time

To determine the best time to pick your crop, see the special feature on pages 72–73. Then begin the processing steps, following directions on the charts, pages 47–49.

When precooking the vegetables, try to use only the amount of water needed to fill the jar after the vegetable has been inserted. Since cooking in liquid leaches vitamins and minerals out of the vegetables, the cooking liquid holds a lot of nutrients and should be saved when possible.

Most vegetables can be canned without salt. Artichokes are an exception; they require an acid-brine solution (see chart on page 47).

4) Fill jars quickly but don't pack them too tight-

ly. Leave head space in jars as indicated on the charts on pages 47–49 or in each recipe

Don't pack jar too tightly

(to within ½ to ¾ inch of jar top is a general rule). Run a long spatula around the jar between food and jar sides, gently releasing any air bubbles (see illustration on page 10). Refill with liquid, if necessary.

5) Stand filled jars in very hot water while you fill the remaining jars (a regular canning kettle full of hot water works nicely). Wipe jar rim with damp cloth to remove any food particles that might prevent a good seal. Remove a jar lid from the hot water and place it on a jar (if lids stick together, plunge in cold water, then hot). Screw ring bands on by hand as tightly as you comfortably can.

6) Before canning the jars of vegetables, you'll need to vent the pressure canner to eliminate all air inside. Place jars on the rack in canner, spaced so they aren't touching the canner or each other. Fasten down the canner lid, leaving the petcock open (or the vent pipe uncovered) and let a jet of steam escape for at least 10 minutes. Air left in the canner will prevent

Vent for 10 minutes

the temperature from rising as high as necessary for canning, causing uneven heat distribution. Spoiling may result, making the food unsafe to eat.

7) After venting the canner, close the petcock or put on the weighted gauge and bring the canner to the required pressure level (see charts on pages 47–49). Process for the length of time indicated in the vegetable canning chart on pages 47–49. Make sure the pressure gauge never falls below the required level. Regulate the element to maintain heat at this correct pressure. Check the altitude note at the end of the chart on page 49 if you are not canning at sea level.

8) After processing, remove canner from the heat to another range element—never to a cold surface. *Be careful* not to tilt the canner; it will be heavy.

9) About 2 minutes after the pressure has returned to zero on the gauge, slowly open the petcock (or remove the weighted gauge).

10) Allow the canner to cool 15 minutes after opening the petcock.

11) Remove the lid by opening the canner away from you so you don't get steam in your face. Let the jars cool in the canner 10 to 15 minutes before being removed. Be careful not to disturb the jars.

12) Remove jars with a jar lifter at the end of the cooling time (see illustration on page 10). You will notice bubbling going on in the jars. This indicates they have a good seal and the contents are still boiling under the vacuum.

13) Set on a folded cloth or board—never on a cold surface. Leave enough room between the jars for air to circulate. When jars are cool, remove ring bands, if desired. To loosen a band that sticks, cover with a hot, damp cloth for 1 to 2 minutes; then loosen.

14) Test for a good seal by pressing the lid with your finger. If it stays down when pressed, the jar is sealed (see illustration on page 10). If the lid pops back up when pressed, it is not sealed.
If the jar didn't seal, refrigerate and use within 24 hours—if food looks and smells all right. Or if you want to recan it, be aware that much of the food value and flavor will be lost, since you must process the jar again for the full length of time. It will be safe to eat, though, if it seals on the second try. Never reuse a lid once it's been used as it won't seal.

15) If, for some reason, you didn't follow the above directions in every detail, be aware of food poisoning by reading the information below on botulism and following directions given.

Guard against botulism

If you have carefully followed the directions just given for canning vegetables in a steam pressure canner and if you've used fresh, not overripe, foods, there's little or no chance of food spoilage. However, a deadly form of food spoilage called *botulism* can occur when low-acid vegetables, meats, poultry, and fish are canned by any method except the steam pressure canner one.

Botulism poisoning occurs when food is eaten that contains toxins produced by the bacterium *Clostridium botulinum*. It is generally fatal. The spores are extremely resistant to heat and grow without oxygen in jars of canned, low-acid foods.

Unfortunately, because this kind of spoilage cannot be seen and sometimes has no odor, it's not easy to detect. But there are signs to watch for: *do not even taste* food from jars showing signs of gas pressure or food that looks mushy, moldy, or gives off a disagreeable odor when opened. If the food seems to look all right but you have doubts about the contents or are unsure how closely you followed the canning steps, *do not taste it*. Get rid of food from a jar with a bulging or corroded lid, or food that has any oozing from under the lid. (Do not buy cans of food that are swollen or leaking. Take the jars to the store manager as suspect and report them to your local health authorities.)

Bulging or corroded lid

Oozing food

Mushy or moldy looking food

Signs of gas pressure (*bubbles*)

Disagreeable odor

It is important that you use only fresh, firm, thoroughly washed vegetables. Use only fresh meats, fish, and poultry. Can vegetables as soon as possible after they are picked. Use a steam pressure canner with an accurate gauge for canning, being careful not to process for less than the required time at the correct temperature. Again, even if you have no doubt about the contents of the jar, heat the food to boiling and then hard simmer (205° to 210° F) for 15 minutes (20 minutes for any greens and cream-style corn). Add 10 minutes for each additional 1,000 feet above sea level. The odor of botulism spoilage may be given off when the food is boiling. It is an odor of decomposition smelling rancid, sour, or cheesy.

To get rid of suspect food, boil it for at least 10 minutes; then flush it down the toilet (boiling prevents contamination of the water supply). Boil the jar, lid, and ring band in strong detergent and water, completely covered, for ½ hour. Dispose of jar, band, and lid. Wash your hands—and anything else that might have come into contact with the contamination—in a bleach solution and rinse thoroughly.

Symptoms of botulism poisoning usually begin within 12 to 36 hours after consumption. They are double vision, inability to swallow, speech difficulty, and progressive paralysis of the respiratory system. Despite available antitoxins, most people affected with botulism die because they do not get medical treatment fast enough. Early symptoms are often overlooked, or not recognized.

Here are some canning cautions to help you guard against botulism:

1. Don't take shortcuts or experiment in home canning. Use only tested, approved methods.

2. Use only jars and lids made especially for home canning. Never use ordinary jars, such as mayonnaise jars.

3. Do not reuse sealing lids. Once the sealant on the lids is broken after having been sealed, it is ineffective for sealing again. Buy new lids.

4. Do not use overripe food. The chemical composition of produce changes with age, losing acidity. It will affect its safety for canning. This is especially true of tomatoes. Make sure the produce is of good quality, with no bruises or soft spots.

5. Do not overpack foods. Trying to get too much food into one jar may result in underprocessing and spoilage.

6. Follow exactly the time and temperature specifications listed in instructions. Adjust processing time according to altitude.

7. Test the seal according to instructions.

8. Do not use canned food that shows signs of spoilage. Watch for bulging lids, leaks, off-odors, off-colors, or mold.

9. Always heat home canned low-acid vegetables or low-acid foods (meat, poultry, and fish) to boiling and then hard simmer (205° to 210° F) for 15 minutes before tasting or serving.

Canning Vegetables in an Acid Solution

Artichokes must be canned in an acid solution. Asparagus, beets, carrots, and summer squash also are suitable for canning this way. Greens are more difficult to can by this method and should be packed loosely in jars and covered generously with the acid solution. You can combine beans or corn with tomatoes, adding acid as directed below; corn alone has a poor flavor.

Snip green bean pods; shell peas; cut asparagus to the length of the jar; trim artichokes and remove outer leaves (bracts); peel and dice carrots and beets. Trim and thoroughly wash spinach and other leafy vegetables. Precook corn on the cob for 10 minutes in boiling water; then cut from the cob. Dice summer squash (flat pieces may mat and heat slowly).

To prepare the acid solution, use 2 quarts water and 1 tablespoon salt with either 1½ cups lemon juice strained through cheesecloth (if using Meyer lemons, use 3 cups lemon juice) or 2⅔ cups vinegar (4% acidity) or 2 cups vinegar (5% acidity). Use a well-known brand of vinegar—not homemade, because it may not contain enough acid. Never use less than the amount called for. Use more acid for peas and leafy vegetables—2 cups lemon juice or 3 cups vinegar (5% acidity) or 4 cups vinegar (4% acidity). Three or four tablespoons of sugar will improve the flavor of peas. Use 3 cups lemon juice or 5⅓ cups vinegar (4% acidity) or 4 cups vinegar (5% acidity) for artichokes.

Place the prepared vegetables in a saucepan. Cover well with the acid liquid or use about 1½ cups liquid to 1 pound prepared vegetables.

Boil over direct heat 5 to 10 minutes, counting time from when boiling begins. Pack the boiling hot vegetables into hot jars (use nothing larger than quart-size) being careful not to pack them too tightly. Cover with the boiling hot cooking liquid, filling to within ½ inch of jar rim. Pack corn and peas filling to within 1 inch of rim. Stand filled jars in the canner of very hot water while filling the other jars. Put lids and ring bands on jar, tightening bands as is comfortably possible. Process following steps 6-7 on pages 44-45 for canning vegetables.

Canning Guide for Vegetables

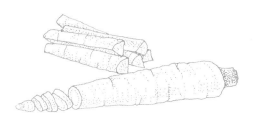

Vegetables	To yield 1 quart (pounds)	How to prepare	Processing time at 10 pounds pressure in minutes: Pints	quarts
Artichoke hearts	35 to 40 1¼-inch or 20 to 30 2-inch, trimmed whole artichokes	Cut off tops 1¼ to 2 inches. Trim outer leaves to nonfibrous heart. Precook for 5 minutes in boiling water to which ¾ cup vinegar per gallon has been added. Drain, discard cooking liquid. Pack hot into jars. Do not overfill. Cover with a boiling brine prepared by adding ¾ cup vinegar or lemon juice and 3 tablespoons salt to 1 gallon water. Fill to within ½ inch of tops of pint or quart jars. Seal.	25	25
Asparagus	2¼ to 4½ lbs.	Wash and cut off scales (bracts). Cut whole stalks into lengths ¾ inch shorter than jar or cut into 1 to 2-inch pieces. Precook whole stalks or cut pieces in boiling water for 1 to 3 minutes to wilt, then plunge quickly into cold water. For whole pack, gather a bundle of stalks with cut ends down and pack (not too tightly) into jars. Or fill to neck of jars with cut pieces. Add salt (use ½ teaspoon for pints, 1 teaspoon for quarts); then add boiling water or cooking liquid to ½ inch of jar tops. Seal.	28	32
Beans, fresh limas	3 to 5 lbs.	Hull and rinse beans. *To pack hot,* precook in a small amount of boiling water until skins wrinkle (1 to 4 minutes). Pack hot beans loosely into jars to within 1 inch of pint jar tops (1½ inches for quarts). Add salt (½ teaspoon for pint jars, 1 teaspoon for quarts); then add boiling water or cooking liquid to cover beans, leaving ½ to ¾ inch head space. Seal. *To pack raw,* follow above directions, omitting precooking steps.	40	50
Beans, green	1½ to 2½ lbs.	Sort and snip or string, if necessary. Leave whole or cut into 1 to 1½-inch pieces. *To pack hot,* precook whole or cut beans in boiling water until pliable (2 to 5 minutes). Pack hot into jars, standing the whole beans on ends or packing cut beans up to jar shoulder. Add salt (½ teaspoon for pint jars, 1 teaspoon for quarts). Cover beans in each jar with boiling water or cooking liquid, leaving ½ to ¾ inch head space. Seal. *To pack raw,* use pieces cut no larger than 1 inch. Pack tightly into jars up to jar shoulders. Add salt and boiling liquid as directed for hot pack.	25 20	30 25
Beets	2½ to 3½ lbs.	Scrub, don't peel. Leave on roots and 1 to 1½ inches of tops. Parboil until skins slip off (about 15 minutes). Dip in cold water. Peel, trim, and slice. Discard woody beets. Reheat in small amount of water. Pack hot into jars filling jars to shoulders. Add ½ teaspoon salt to pint jars; 1 teaspoon to quarts. Cover beets with the boiling liquid in which the beets were reheated. Add boiling water if needed. Seal.	35	40
Broccoli		Not recommended for canning.		
Brussels Sprouts		Not recommended for canning.		
Cabbage		Not recommended for home canning.		
Carrots	2 to 3 lbs.	Wash and peel or scrape. Cut in slices or cut lengthwise into strips that are 1 inch shorter than jars. Pack raw slices into jars up to shoulder or pack strips lengthwise	30	30

(Continued on next page)

Vegetables	To yield 1 quart (pounds)	How to prepare	Processing time at 10 pounds pressure in minutes: pints	quarts
Carrots (continued)		to within 1 inch of tops. Add ½ teaspoon salt to pint jars, 1 teaspoon to quarts. Pour in boiling water to cover vegetables, allowing ½ to ¾ inch head space. Seal.		
Cauliflower		Pickle only. Not recommended for canning.		
Celery	1½ to 2½ lbs.	Wash, remove leafy tops and coarse strings. Slice or cut in lengths ¾ to 1 inch shorter than jars.		
		To pack hot, use sliced celery; precook 1 to 3 minutes, depending on size and tenderness. Pack hot into jars up to jar shoulders.	35	35
		Add ½ teaspoon salt to pints, 1 teaspoon to quarts. Cover with cooking liquid or boiling water, leaving about ½ inch head space. Seal.		
		To pack raw, pack slices loosely up to jar shoulder or arrange long pieces upright in jars. Add salt and water as directed for hot pack. Seal.	30	30
Corn	3 to 6 lbs. (8 to 16 ears)	Plan to can corn as soon as possible after harvest. Remove husks and silk.		
		For whole kernel corn, use a sharp knife to cut raw kernels from cob to ⅔ of total depth. Do not scrape the cobs. In a pan, cover corn with brine made by adding 1 tablespoon salt to each quart water. Heat to boiling, then pack hot into jars to within 1 inch of jar tops, covering corn in jars with brine. Seal.	55	70
		For cream-style corn, cut corn off cob the same as for whole kernel corn, then scrape the cobs, being careful not to scrape off any of the cob material. Cover with brine made from 1 teaspoon salt to each quart of water; proceed as for whole kernel corn; leave 1¼ inches head space in pint jars when packed with mixture of corn and brine (don't use quart jars).	85	
Cucumbers		Not recommended for canning.		
Eggplant		Not recommended for canning.		
Greens: spinach, swiss chard, beet greens, other greens		Not recommended for home canning.		
Kohlrabi		Not recommended for canning.		
Mushrooms	1½ lbs.	Trim stems and discolored parts. Soak in cold water 10 minutes; wash to clean. Leave small mushrooms whole; cut larger ones in half or quarter. Place in a steamer over boiling water and steam 4 minutes or heat gently 15 minutes in a covered saucepan without liquid. Pack hot mushrooms into jars to jar shoulders. Add ¼ teaspoon salt to half pints; ½ teaspoon to pints. Add boiling hot cooking liquid or water to cover mushrooms, leaving ½ inch space at top (don't use quart jars). Seal.	30	
Onions, small white		Peel. An easy way to remove skins is to pour boiling water over onions; let stand 2 to 3 minutes, drain, and peel. Precook for 5 minutes in boiling water to which ¾ cup vinegar per gallon has been added. Drain, saving cooking liquid. Pack hot into jars to jar shoulders. Cover with cooking liquid to which 3 tablespoons salt per gallon is added. Leave ½ inch head space. Seal.	25	25
Parsnips		Not recommended for canning.		
Peas	3 to 6 lbs.	Shell and wash, using tender, young peas.		
		To pack hot, can only young, tender peas. Hull and precook for 1 to 4 minutes in a small amount of water until the skins wrinkle. Pack hot into jars to within 1¼ inches of tops. Add ½ teaspoon salt for pint jars; 1 teaspoon salt for quarts. Cover to within 1 inch of jar tops with the boiling liquid in which the peas were cooked. Add boiling	40	45

(Continued on next page)

Vegetables	To yield 1 quart (pounds)	How to prepare	Processing time at 10 pounds pressure in minutes: pints	quarts
Peas (continued)		water if needed. Seal. *To pack raw,* pack loosely to within 1 inch of jar tops. Add salt as for hot pack. Cover with boiling water leaving ¾ inch head space. Seal.	40	45
Peppers, bell (green and red) and Pimiento	2 to 3 lbs.	Cut out the stem end of each pepper and remove the core and seeds. Place in a shallow pan in a 450° oven until the skins separate. Chill at once in cold water and peel. Pack cooled peppers into jars to jar shoulders. Add ½ teaspoon salt and ½ tablespoon lemon juice to pint jars, 1 teaspoon salt and 1 tablespoon lemon juice to quart jars. Cover with boiling water, leaving ½ inch head space. Seal. *Process peppers at only 5 pounds pressure as higher pressures affect texture and flavor.* Process pints for 50 minutes, quarts for 60 minutes.	See information under "How to prepare"	
Potatoes, new	4 to 6 lbs.	Scrape the peel off new potatoes. Leave small ones whole; cut larger ones in halves. Pack raw into jars to jar shoulders. Pour over boiling brine made by adding 1½ to 2 tablespoons salt to 1 quart water, leaving ½ inch head space. Seal.	35	40
Potatoes, Sweet	2 to 3 lbs.	Wash and remove any blemishes. *To pack dry,* place in steamer over boiling water or boil in a quantity of water until partially soft (20 to 30 minutes). Peel and cut in pieces if large. Pack tightly into jars, pressing to fill spaces. Add no salt or liquid. Seal.	65	95
		To pack wet, steam or boil as for dry pack, except remove as soon as skins slip off easily. Peel, cut in pieces, and pack hot into jars to within 1 inch of tops. Add ½ teaspoon salt to pint jars, 1 teaspoon salt to quarts. Cover potatoes with boiling water or a medium syrup (see syrups on page 8), leaving ¾ inch head space. Seal.	55	90
Rutabaga		Not recommended for canning.		
Spinach		Not recommended for canning.		
Squash, Summer (crookneck, zucchini, pattypan)	1½ lbs.	Wash and trim ends, don't peel. Cut into uniform ½-inch thick slices. *To pack hot,* put into a pan, add water to just cover, and bring to boiling. Pack hot into jars, filling loosely up to jar shoulders. Add ½ teaspoon salt to pints, 1 teaspoon to quarts. Cover squash with boiling cooking liquid, leaving ½ inch head space at top. Seal.	30	40
		To pack raw, pack slices tightly into jars to within 1 inch of tops. Add salt as for hot pack, then fill jars with boiling liquid, leaving ½ inch head space. Seal.	25	30
Squash, Winter (pumpkin, banana, hubbard, butternut)	1½ to 3 lbs.	Cut through rind; cut flesh into strips, scraping out all fibrous material and seeds. Place in a steamer over boiling water or boil in a small amount of water until flesh is soft. Scrape flesh from rind and press through a colander or mash. Put into a pan and bring to boiling, stirring. Pack hot into jars to within ½ to ¾ inch of jar tops. Add ½ teaspoon salt to pint jars, 1 teaspoon to quarts. Seal.	85	115
Tomatoes (see under Guide to Fruit Canning on page 13)				
Turnips	2 to 3 lbs.	Wash and peel or scrape. Cut in uniform ¼-inch slices or about ½-inch dice. Pack raw into jars filling up to jar shoulders. Add ½ teaspoon salt to pint jars, 1 teaspoon to quarts. Pour in boiling water to cover, allowing ½ to ¾ inch head space. Seal.	30	30

Note: At altitudes higher than sea level, increase pressure 1 pound for the first 1,000 foot increase in elevation and ½ pound for each additional 1,000 feet. Times remain the same for processing.

Vegetable Recipes

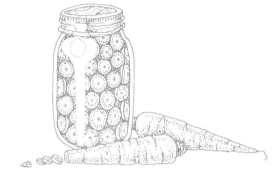

Squash with Apples

Families who enjoy spicy, fruit-flavored squash, might like to can it already flavored. To serve, reheat, and sprinkle with toasted sliced almonds. For each quart, you'll need the following proportions.

> **About 1 pound winter squash, seeded and peeled**
> 1 **large Golden Delicious apple, peeled**
> 4 **tablespoons butter or margarine**
> ¼ **cup water**
> ¼ **cup lemon juice or vinegar**
> ¼ **cup firmly packed brown sugar**
> ¼ **teaspoon ground cinnamon**
> ⅛ **teaspoon ground nutmeg**
> **About ¼ teaspoon salt**

Cut the squash and apple into ½-inch cubes; you should have about 4 cups. Melt the butter in a wide frying pan over medium heat. Add the squash, apple, water, and lemon juice. Stir. Cover and cook, stirring occasionally, until tender. Stir in sugar, cinnamon, nutmeg, and salt to taste. Mash squash.

To pressure can, follow steps 1-2 on page 44; then continue with steps 4-15, processing quarts for 1 hour and 55 minutes. Makes 1 quart.

Corn Chowder

Serve this hearty Corn Chowder on a winter evening. You might add a little butter when you reheat the chowder before serving, and sprinkle each serving with crumbled, crisp bacon.

> 2 **tablespoons bacon drippings or butter**
> 1 **large onion, diced**
> 1 **quart water**
> 4 **cups diced, peeled potatoes**
> 4 **cups cream-style corn (prepared as directed on page 47)**
> 1 **quart milk (or 1 pt. each milk and half-and-half)**
> **About 3 teaspoons salt**
> **About ½ teaspoon seasoned pepper**

In a Dutch oven (at least 5-quart size) heat drippings or butter over medium heat. Add onion and sauté until limp. Add water, potatoes, and corn. Cover and simmer about 20 minutes. Add milk, season to taste with salt and seasoned pepper, and reheat to simmering.

To pressure can, prepare 5 pint jars and other canning equipment following steps 1-2 on page 44. Pour hot chowder into jars to about ½ inch of jar rims. Then follow steps 5-15, processing pint jars 1 hour and 40 minutes at 10 pounds pressure (canning in quart jars not recommended). Makes 5 pints.

Refried Beans

Traditionally, refried beans go into many Mexican dishes. They are economical and tasty accompanying or filling tacos, enchiladas, and tostadas.

You can put up your own refried beans using a pressure canner. Just reheat the beans slowly, stirring, to serve.

> 1 **pound dried pinto or pink beans, cleaned**
> 5 **cups water**
> 1 **or 2 medium-sized onions, diced (optional)**
> ½ **to 1 cup hot bacon drippings, butter, or lard**
> **Salt to taste**

Combine beans in a pan with water and onions. Bring to a boil, cover, and remove from heat for 2 hours (or soak beans in cold water overnight). Return to heat, bring to a boil, and simmer slowly until beans are very tender (about 3 hours). Mash beans with a potato masher and add bacon drippings, butter or lard. Mix well; continue cooking, stirring frequently until beans are thickened and fat is absorbed. Salt to taste. Serve, reheat, or can. Makes 6 to 8 servings.

To pressure can, prepare 3 pint jars and other canning equipment following steps 1 and 2 on page 44. Fill jars with hot beans, leaving about ½ inch head space; follow steps 5-15, processing pints or quarts 1 hour and 45 minutes at 10 pounds pressure. Makes 3 pints.

Western Succotash

If you enjoy this vegetable combination, why not can the corn and beans together? To serve, drain and reheat, adding butter and about ¼ cup whipping cream to each pint or to taste.

1 quart whole-kernel corn
1 quart precooked fresh limas or green beans
½ cup finely chopped onion
  About 1 cup water
  Salt

Prepare corn as directed on the chart on page 47, heating it to the boiling point in brine; then re-move with a slotted spoon. Also precook the fresh limas or green beans as directed on the chart on page 47. Meanwhile, prepare 4 pint or 2 quart jars and other canning equipment following steps 1–2 on page 44.

To pressure can, combine corn, limas or beans, onion, and water; heat to boiling. Pack hot into jars, filling to shoulders of jars. Add ½ teaspoon salt to each pint. Add the cooking liquid and water, if necessary, to cover vegetables in jars. Then follow steps 5–15, processing pints 1 hour or quarts 1 hour and 30 minutes at 10 pounds pressure. Makes 5 pints. See introduction for serving suggestions.

Canning Meats, Poultry, & Seafood

If you've raised a prize steer for the county fair or have purchased a side of beef for the winter, you may be facing storage problems. Freezing, of course, is the easiest method for keeping meats, poultry, and fish fresh; but if you do not have a freezer, consider canning. (Frozen meats also may be defrosted and canned at home.)

Meats to can are beef, veal, lamb, pork, chicken, turkey, rabbit, game birds, and small and large game animals. Fishermen are invited to consider the canning techniques on pages 53-54.

Meat, poultry, and fish canned at home must be processed in a steam pressure canner. To destroy potentially dangerous bacteria in meats, a temperature of 240° F must be held for a specific length of time. This temperature can only be attained under pressure in a steam pressure canner.

Never think of processing meat in a regular canning kettle using boiling water method safe for canning fruits and tomatoes, in an oven, in a steamer without pressure, a regular pressure cooker for fast cooking, or in an open canning kettle. Botulism food poisoning is a real danger in all these cases (for more information on botulism, see pages 45–46).

If you are slaughtering your own animals, chill the meat immediately afterwards to prevent spoilage and permit tenderizing. The meat is much easier to handle when it is cold. Keep meat at a temperature below 40° F until time to can it. Can within a few days of slaughter.

If refrigeration is not available and if the maximum daily temperature is above 40° F, process meat as soon as the animal's body heat is gone. If the meat must be held for more than a few days, freeze it and store at 0° F or below. Before canning, cut or saw frozen meat into pieces of desired size and thaw in the refrigerator at 40° F or lower until the ice crystals have gone. Always keep all meat clean. Rinse poultry thoroughly in cold water and drain before canning.

If you catch your own fish, can or freeze it as soon as possible. Immediately clean and chill it after the catch. Chill until you are ready to preserve it. If no refrigeration is handy, rub it with a salt mixture or cover with a wet cloth.

Equipment you'll need to can meat and poultry

All equipment that may come in contact with the meat should be scrubbed with soapy hot water. The canning equipment for meat is the same as for vegetables. The steam pressure canner is the essential piece of equipment. Read carefully the information under *Equipment you'll need* on page 43. Also helpful is an accurate, mercury-type thermometer for measuring the temperature in the packed, unsealed jars of food.

Two ways to pack meat and poultry into jars

Before you can begin processing meat and poultry, it must be packed properly into canning jars using one of the two methods below.

The hot-pack method requires the meat and poultry to be precooked before it is packed into canning jars, usually until medium-done. Pack hot meat into jars. Pour boiling broth or water over the meat in the jar. Salt may be added for flavor but doesn't act as a preservative. The temperature of the meat in the jar at the time it is sealed should be 170°.

The raw-pack method starts by packing uncooked meat into the canning jars. Then the open jars are placed on a rack in a large pan of boiling water (the canning kettle used without pressure gauge is good for this). The water should be about 2 inches below the tops of the jars. Cover the kettle and simmer until the temperature in the center of the food inside the jars is 170° (check with a thermometer). This exhausts the air from the jars and creates a vacuum in the jars after sealing and processing. It also helps prevent changes in flavor.

Exhaust air from jars

Step-by-step canning for meat and poultry

1) Have ready the steam pressure canner (see under *Equipment you'll need* on page 43), jars, lids, ring bands, and other canning accessories (see page 7). Canning jars and ring bands need to be clean. Check jars for nicks or cracks that might prevent a good seal (see illustration on page 9). Discard these and any rusted or bent ring bands. Scald lids just before using and keep in very hot water.

2) Place the rack in the steam pressure canner and put 2 to 3 inches of hot water in the canner bottom (enough to keep it from boiling dry). The water can come to within 2 inches of the jar tops (see illustration below left). Cover canner to bring water to a boil, keeping it hot while preparing the meat.

3) Prepare the meat, following directions on chart on page 55, and referring to one of the two methods for packing meat into jars given left. Wipe the rim of packed jar to remove any fat or meat particles that might prevent a proper seal. Seal lids by screwing on ring bands as tight as is comfortable.

4) Set packed jars on the rack in the steam pressure canner, allowing space for steam to flow around each jar. If using two layers of jars, stagger top layer on a rack placed between the layers, making sure none of the jars is touching another.

5) Fasten canner cover securely so steam only comes out through the petcock or weighted-gauge opening. Let a jet of steam escape for at least 10 minutes. This will drive all the air from the canner. Air left in the canner will prevent the temperature from becoming as high as necessary and will cause uneven heat distribution. Close petcock or put on weighted gauge after 10 minutes of venting.

6) Let pressure rise to 10 pounds (240°F). Then immediately start counting the processing time. Regulate the heat under the canner to maintain an even pressure. Do not lower pressure by opening the petcock. Keep drafts from reaching the canner. Fluctuating pressure during the processing causes liquid to be drawn out of the jars. Watch timing carefully. When time is up, immediately remove canner from heat to another range element—never to a cold surface. Let canner stand until pressure drops to zero. Never pour cold water over canner to hasten the process; the jars lose liquid if there's a sudden drop in temperature.

7) At zero, wait a minute or two; then slowly open petcock or take off weighted gauge. Unfasten cover and tilt the far side up so steam escapes away from you. Take jars from canner with a jar lifter or tongs (see illustration on page 10). Place on a cloth or board to cool, keeping away from drafts. Don't cover jars.

8) When cool, take off ring bands. Loosen stuck bands by covering them with a hot, damp cloth. Check for any leaks and a good seal. To check seal, press on center of lid; if lid stays down, it's sealed (see illustration on page 10). Refrigerate and use food immediately from any leaky jar or can it again in another jar and new lid following heating steps from the beginning and processing for a full second time.

Loss of liquid doesn't cause canned meat to spoil; never try to refill jars that have lost liquid during the canning process. Store jars in a cool, dry place. Heat causes a loss in food quality.

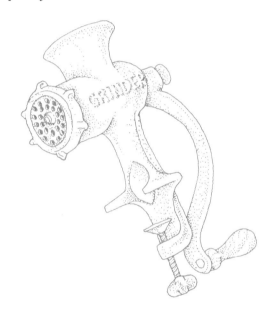

Be aware of spoilage

Freezing doesn't spoil jars of canned meats but may damage the lid seal so that spoilage can begin. If you store jars in an unheated area, such as a storage shed, where temperatures drop to freezing, cover the jars with a blanket or wrap them in newspapers. Dampness may corrode jar lids and cause leakage.

Signs of spoilage may show up when you take jars of meat from storage. Bulging jar lids or ring bands, gas bubbles, or leaks all indicate that seals have broken and the food has spoiled. Also check jar contents as you open the lid. Spurting liquid, off-odor, and color changes in meats are danger signs. Sulfur in meat often causes metal lids or cans to darken. This discoloration does not affect the safety of the meat.

Boiling is the best way to find out if canned meat is safe to eat. Heating brings out the characteristic odor of spoiled meat. Always destroy bad-smelling meat without even tasting it. Read the information on botulism on pages 45-46 if you have any questions about whether the meat is safe to eat or not. *Always* heat home-canned meat to boiling and then hard simmer (205° to 210° F) for 15 minutes in a covered pan before tasting or using.

Step-by-step canning for fish

1) Have ready a steam pressure canner (see under *Equipment you'll need,* page 43), jars, lids, ring bands, and other canning accessories (pages 5–7). Canning jars and ring bands must be clean. Check jars for nicks or cracks. Discard these and any rusted ring bands. Scald lids before using, keeping in very hot water until used.

2) Place the rack in the pressure canner and pour 2 to 3 inches of hot water into the canner bottom (enough to keep it from boiling dry). The water can come to within 2 inches of the jar tops. Cover canner to bring water to a boil and keep it hot while preparing the fish.

3) Scale salmon and other large-scaled fish with a fish-scaling knife or other knife with a dull blade. Scrape from tail to head. Skin tuna.

Remove fins and clean fish thoroughly. Cut off the head and tail. Wash the body cavities thoroughly.

Split fish lengthwise along backbone. Remove backbone, leaving as little flesh as possible on bone.

4) Cut fish (except tuna) into pieces the length of the jar. Soak pieces in a brine made of ¾ cup salt mixed with 1 gallon water for 1 hour (this amount is sufficient for 25 pounds of cleaned fish). Or, if you don't soak the fish in brine, add salt to jars after packing.

Pack jars as full as possible with fish, arranging the pieces with skin sides next to jar sides, alternating head and tail ends if packing small fish. If you soak fish in brine, don't add water to jars. If fish wasn't soaked in brine, add at least 1 teaspoon salt to each pint jar, then fill to brim with water.

5) Wipe jar rims with a damp cloth, removing any particles that might prevent a proper seal. Seal lid by screwing on ring band as tight as is comfortably possible.

6) Place jars on the rack in the pressure canner, allowing space for steam to flow around each jar. If using two layers of jars, stagger top layer on a rack placed between the layers, making sure none of the jars are touching.

7) Fasten canner cover securely so steam only comes out through the petcock or weighted-gauge opening. Let steam escape for at least 10 minutes. This will drive all air from the canner. Air left in the canner will prevent the temperature from rising as high as is necessary and will cause uneven heat distribution. Close petcock or put on weighted gauge after 10 minutes of venting.

8) Let pressure rise to 10 pounds pressure (240° F). Then immediately start counting the processing time of 1 hour and 50 minutes. Regulate the heat under the canner to maintain an even pressure. Keep drafts from reaching the canner. Fluctuating pressure during the processing causes liquid to be drawn out of the jars. Watch timing carefully. Remove canner immediately from heat when time is up. Place on another range element—never on a cold surface. Let canner stand until pressure drops to zero. Never pour cold water over canner to hasten the process. The jars lose liquid if there's a sudden drop in temperature.

9) At zero, wait a minute or two; then slowly open petcock or take off weighted gauge. Unfasten cover and tilt the far side up so steam escapes away from you. Take jars from canner. Place on a cloth or board to cool, keeping away from drafts. Don't cover jars.

10) When cool, take off ring bands. Check for leaks and seal. Press center of lid; if lid stays down, it's sealed. If jar is not sealed, refrigerate and use immediately or can it again using another jar and new lid, following heating steps from the beginning and processing for a full second time. Store in a cool, dry place. Heat causes a loss of quality. (See information on spoilage on page 53.)

Canning precooked tuna

1) Rub all surfaces of cleaned fish, including the cavities, with salad oil.

2) Precook fish by steaming 2 to 4 hours, depending on the size of the fish, or cook in a covered pan in a 350° oven for about 1 hour. Cook until the blood along the backbone has set and is no longer pink.

3) Cool fish in the refrigerator until firm enough to handle easily.

4) Get out canning equipment, following steps 1-2 under *Step-by-step canning for fish,* page 53.

5) Split fish lengthwise and remove backbone.

6) Skin and break lengthwise into quarters.

Scrape away all dark meat.

7) Cut pieces into lengths ⅜ inch shorter than the length of the canning jar. Pack fish into containers; fill any spaces with broken pieces of fish.

8) Add ½ teaspoon salt to pint-sized jars, ¼ teaspoon to half-pint sized jars.

9) In a saucepan, heat salad oil (or use boiling water), making sure to keep the oil below the smoking point. Add 2 to 4 tablespoons hot oil to each pint, 1 to 2 tablespoons to each half-pint.

10) Seal jars, following steps 5-10 under *Step-by step canning for fish,* page 53. Process at 10 pounds pressure (240° F) for 2 hours.

Canning smoked fish

Smoked fish should be canned immediately after smoking and cooling it. Cut fish into pieces the length of the jars. Pack jars as full as possible with the fish. Don't add salt or water. Seal jars, and process, following steps 5-10 under *Step-by-step canning for fish,* page 53. Process 2 hours at 10 pounds pressure (240° F.).

Using Canned Salmon

Cooking proceeds at a fast pace here, so have all vegetables cut and the sauce ready before starting.

Drain 1 can (1 lb.) or 1 pint home-canned salmon and carefully separate into large chunks, discarding bones and skin. Heat home-canned salmon to 210°F for 15 minutes before using. Warm store-purchase, canned salmon in an oven just to heat.

Heat 2 tablespoons salad oil in a frying pan over medium-high heat. Add ½ medium-sized onion (cut in about 1-inch squares), 1 medium-sized carrot (cut in slanting slices ¼ inch thick), and 1 small clove garlic (minced or mashed); cook, turning with a spatula, for about 3 minutes or until vegetables are slightly tender but still crisp. Add ½ medium-sized green pepper (seeded and cut in 1-inch squares), ½ cup canned pineapple chunks (drained), about 12 cherry tomatoes (halved), and the Sweet and Sour Sauce (recipe follows). Cook, turning until mixture boils and thickens (about 1 minute). Spoon mixture over salmon. Serves 4.

Sweet and Sour Sauce. Blend 1½ teaspoons cornstarch with 3 tablespoons brown sugar and stir in ⅛ teaspoon ground ginger, 2 teaspoons each soy sauce and Sherry, and 2 tablespoons each wine vinegar and water.

Canning Guide
for Meats & Poultry

Meat	Directions	Processing time at 10 pounds pressure in minutes: pints	quarts
Meat, cut-up	Cut meat from bone, trimming away most fat without unduly slashing lean part of meat. Cut tender meat in strips about 1 inch shorter than jars so grain runs lengthwise. Cut less tender pieces in chunks as for stew.		
	Hot pack; put meat in large shallow pan; add just enough water to keep from sticking. Cover pan. Precook slowly until medium-done. Stir occasionally for even heat distribution. Pack hot meat loosely into jars, leaving 1 inch space at top. Add salt, if desired (½ teaspoon to pints, 1 teaspoon to quarts). Cover meat with boiling meat broth, adding boiling water if needed. Adjust lids. Seal.	75	90
	Raw pack; pack raw meat loosely into jars, leaving 1 inch head-space. Place open jars in kettle of boiling water and heat slowly until temperature in center of food inside jars is 170° (see page 52). Without a thermometer, heat 75 minutes. Add salt as for hot pack. Seal.	75	90
Meat, ground	Use small pieces of fresh, clean lean meat, never mixing leftover scraps or lumps of fat with fresh meat. Add 1 teaspoon of salt for each pound of ground meat, mixing well.		
	Shape ground meat into fairly thin patties that can be packed into jars without breaking. Precook patties in a 325° oven until medium done (so almost no red color shows when cut in center). Skim all fat off, do not use in canning. Pack into jars leaving 1 inch space above meat. Cover with boiling meat broth to 1 inch of top of jars. Adjust jar lids. Seal.	75	90
Sausage	Use your favorite sausage recipe but go lightly on seasonings as they change flavor in canning and storage. (Omit sage as it makes canned sausage bitter.) Shape into patties, precook, pack, and process as directed for ground meat above.	75	90
Stock, Beef or Chicken	*Hot pack;* make stock fairly concentrated: Cover bony pieces of meat or chicken with lightly salted water. Simmer until tender. Skim off fat, remove bones, leaving meat in stock. Pour boiling soup stock into jars, leaving 1 inch space at top. Adjust lids. Seal.	20	25
Poultry, cut-up	Debone breast, cut drumsticks off short. Leave bone in other meaty pieces. Trim off fat. Use bony pieces for making broth (see below).		
	Hot pack with bone; place raw in a pan and cover with hot broth or water. Put on lid, heat, stirring occasionally until medium done. To test, cut piece at center; if pink is almost gone, meat is ready. Pack loosely in jars. Place thighs and drumsticks with skin next to glass. Fit breasts into center as well as the other small pieces. Leave 1 inch space above poultry. Add salt if desired (½ teaspoon for pints, 1 teaspoon for quarts). Cover with boiling cooking broth, leaving 1 inch at top of jar. Adjust lids. Seal.	65	75
	Hot pack without bone; remove all bones from poultry (leaving skin) either before or after precooking as above. Pack jars loosely with hot chicken following directions given above, leaving 1 inch space above poultry. Add salt if desired (½ teaspoon for pints, 1 teaspoon for quarts). Pour in boiling broth leaving 1 inch space at top of jar. Adjust lids. Seal.	75	90
	Raw pack with bone; pack raw poultry loosely in jar placing thighs and drumsticks with skin next to glass. Fit breast and small pieces into center. Pack into jars to within 1 inch of top. Simmer poultry in jars until food in center of jar reaches 170°F (see page 52). Without a thermometer, simmer until medium done (about 75 minutes). Add salt if desired (½ teaspoon for pints or 1 teaspoon for quarts). Adjust lids. Seal.	65	75

*To make meat or poultry broth, place bony pieces in a saucepan and cover with cold water. Simmer until meat is tender. Pour broth into another pan; skim off fat. Add boiling broth to canning jars packed with precooked meat or poultry; fill to level specified in directions.

Note: For higher than sea level altitudes, increase pressure by 1 pound for each 2,000 feet. Times remain the same.

Meat Recipes

Traditional Mincemeat

Old-fashioned, do-it-from-scratch cooking has not disappeared in this convenience-food era. Making mincemeat is easy, especially if you have your own beef.

> 2 pounds boneless beef stew meat, cubed
> Water
> 1 pound beef suet, membrane removed
> 1 pound mixed candied fruit peel
> 3 pounds apples, pared, cored, and finely chopped
> 2 pounds firmly packed light brown sugar
> 4 cups cider
> 1 tablespoon each salt, ground nutmeg, allspice, and cloves
> 2 tablespoons ground cinnamon
> 1½ cups light molasses
> 3 packages (11 oz. each) currants
> 1 pound each seedless raisins and golden raisins
> 2 cups brandy (optional)

Cover meat with water and bring to a boil; cook until tender and almost dry (about 1½ hours). Cool the meat; put it through a food chopper, using the medium blade. (You should have about 5½ cups of ground, cooked meat.) Put suet and candied fruit peel through the chopper. Mix with meat, and blend in apples.

Dissolve sugar in cider in a large (8 to 10-quart) pan; bring to a boil. Carefully add the meat mixture to syrup and return to a boil. Reduce heat and simmer about 5 minutes. Remove from heat. Add salt, spices, molasses, currants, and raisins, mixing thoroughly. Blend in the brandy. Cool to room temperature (at this point, you can freeze mincemeat in quart containers).

To pressure can, follow steps 1-8 using the hot-pack method on page 52, processing pints and quarts for 30 minutes. Makes 6 quarts.

Mincemeat Pie. Prepare pastry for a 2-crust, 9-inch pie. Roll out half the pastry and line a 9-inch pie pan. Fill with 1 quart (4 cups) mincemeat. Roll remaining pastry to a rectangle; cut into ¾-inch strips. Alternate pastry strips to make a lattice; seal lattice strips to lower pastry, and flute the edge. Bake in a 425° oven for 35 minutes or until nicely browned.

Meat Sauce for Pasta

This meaty tomato sauce contains lots of vegetables and herbs. To serve, just reheat and spoon over hot, cooked pasta, such as rigatoni, gnocchi, or spaghetti. Top off with grated Parmesan or Romano cheese.

> 2 tablespoons salad oil
> About 12 ounces mild Italian pork sausage (4 medium-sized links)
> 2 medium-sized onions, chopped
> ½ pound lean ground beef
> 2 cloves garlic, minced or mashed
> 2 carrots, finely chopped or grated
> 2 stalks celery, chopped
> ½ pound mushrooms, sliced
> 2 cans (6 oz. each) tomato paste
> 2 quarts home-canned tomatoes or fresh tomatoes, peeled and chopped
> 1 cup dry red wine
> 2 teaspoons basil leaves
> ¼ teaspoon rubbed sage
> 1 cup chopped parsley
> 1 teaspoon salt
> ½ teaspoon pepper

In a 3-quart kettle heat the oil over medium heat. Squeeze the sausage meat from the casing and break it up in the oil. Brown, stirring occasionally. Add the onion and cook until translucent; then add ground beef and brown. Stir in garlic, carrot, celery, and mushrooms, and cook for a minute or two, then add tomato paste, tomatoes (breaking up canned tomatoes with a fork), wine, basil, sage, parsley, salt, and pepper. Turn heat to low, cover, and simmer 1½ to 2 hours or until thickened and flavors are well blended. Skim and discard fat.

To pressure can, follow steps 1-8, pages 52–53, processing pints 1 hour and 5 minutes, quarts 1 hour and 15 minutes. Makes about 5 pints.

Simmered Corned Beef

You cook this corned beef in a flavorful liquid; then let it chill in the cooking liquid before canning.

About 5 pounds corned beef, bottom round or brisket
Water
1 medium-sized onion, chopped
¼ teaspoon each garlic powder and liquid hot pepper seasoning
1 teaspoon dill weed
3 bay leaves
2 sticks whole cinnamon
5 whole cloves
1 whole orange, thinly sliced

Put the corned beef in a Dutch oven; add 2 quarts water. Cover, bring to a boil, reduce heat, and simmer for 30 minutes. Taste water; if salty, pour off meat and add 2 quarts more water to beef.

Stir in the onion, garlic powder, liquid hot pepper seasoning, dill, bay, cinnamon, cloves, and orange slices. Cover and simmer for 2½ to 3 hours or until meat is tender when pierced. Cool, cover, and chill overnight.

Remove meat from broth (save it for making a soup) and slice meat or cut into 1-inch-sized chunks.

To pressure can, follow steps 1-8, pages 52–53, processing pints 1 hour and 15 minutes, quarts 1 hour and 30 minutes. Makes about 4 pints.

Mexican Chile Con Carne

Serve this spicy, meat-filled chile with homemade cornbread or muffins.

1 pound dry pink or red beans
4 pounds beef stew meat, cut in ½-inch cubes
3 tablespoons salad oil
1 large onion, sliced
1 clove garlic, mashed
1 quart home-canned tomatoes or peeled, chopped fresh tomatoes
2½ teaspoons salt
2 teaspoons each chile powder and oregano leaves
½ teaspoon ground cumin

Soak beans overnight in water to cover; or cover them with water, bring to a boil, simmer 2 minutes, and let soak for 1 hour. Drain beans and reserve the liquid. Brown the meat in the oil; then add the soaked beans, the onion, garlic, tomatoes,

salt, chile powder, oregano, cumin, and about 3 cups of the bean liquid. Cover, bring to a boil; simmer gently about 1½ hours, adding more bean liquid as needed.

To pressure can, follow steps 1-8, pages 52–53, processing pints 1 hour 15 minutes, quarts 1 hour 30 minutes. Makes about 3 pints.

Beef and Vegetable Supper Soup

You might offer sour cream at the table to add to individual servings of this whole-meal soup.

3 pounds boneless lean beef, cut in bite-sized pieces
6 cups water
About 2 teaspoons salt
About ½ teaspoon pepper
2 cloves garlic, minced or mashed
1 whole bay leaf
⅓ cup pearl barley or rice
1 quart home canned tomatoes or peeled, chopped fresh tomatoes
4 stalks celery, sliced
4 large carrots, sliced
2 medium-sized onions, cut in wedges
½ small head cabbage, coarsely shredded
2 cans (about 1 lb. each) red kidney beans

In a Dutch oven or other large, heavy pan, combine the meat, water, 2 teaspoons salt, and ½ teaspoon pepper. Bring slowly to a boil, spooning off any scum that rises to the top. Add garlic and bay. Cover and simmer gently until meat is tender (about 1¼ hours).

Add the barley or rice, tomatoes (including liquid), celery, carrots, onion, and cabbage. Cover and simmer until the vegetables are tender (about 20 minutes). Add the beans, including their liquid. Taste, and add more salt and pepper, if needed.

To pressure can, follow steps 1-8, pages 52–53, processing pints 1 hour and 45 minutes, quarts 1 hour and 55 minutes. Makes about 14 pints.

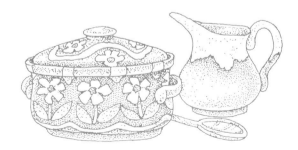

If You Have Questions...

Q. Is it safe to process foods in empty mayonnaise jars or other jars prepared foods come in?

A. No. They may break during processing and you can't get a proper seal using regular canning lids or the jar's own lid.

Q. Is it safe to use the fancy jars from gift stores with wire bands that clamp over lids?

A. Not unless they are specifically for canning and made with tempered glass. If they are not, they may break during processing or you may not be able to get a proper seal.

Q. Must glass jars and their lids be sterilized by boiling water before canning fruits or vegetables?

A. Not if you are using the boiling water method or steam pressure canner method. Both the containers and the food are sterilized during the processing at high heat. Just make sure that the jars, lids, and ring bands are clean and that the lids are hot so they will seal. But sterilize them all if using open-bath canning, as in processing jams and preserves.

Q. What foods use the boiling water method?

A. All fruits, fruit juices, and fruit purées, tomatoes, and pickles

Q. What foods must be canned in a steam pressure canner?

A. All vegetables (except tomatoes and pickles) and all meat, poultry, and fish.

Q. Can I substitute a steam pressure canner for a water-bath canner when processing fruits?

A. Yes. Leave the lid off the steam pressure canner (or ajar) and follow directions for water-bath canning without using the gauge or petcock. Just make sure water covers the jars by at least 1 inch.

Q. Is it safe to reuse canning lids?

A. No. The sealing compound is damaged by first use and won't seal again. Ring bands can be used repeatedly if in good shape.

Q. Can foods be processed in the oven?

A. No. Jars might explode and the temperature of the food in the jars during processing doesn't get high enough to insure bacteria destruction.

Q. Why should ascorbic acid be added to fruit and vegetables?

A. Ascorbic acid is an anti-darkening agent which retards the oxidation that browns foods. It keeps foods looking attractive.

Q. If the ring bands come loose during canning, should they be tightened on the jar afterwards?

A. Tighten sufficiently before canning. It is no use to tighten them after canning, since their purpose is to keep the lid in place and in any case they are taken off after the food is cool.

Q. If I want to use half-pint-sized jars instead of pint-sized jars, how long do I process them?

A. Half pints and pints can be processed the same length of time.

Q. Do fruits have to be canned with sugar?

A. No. Fruit juice, water, or honey may be used instead.

Q. Why not invert jelly glasses as some books recommend?

A. Inverting glasses gives a last heat treatment to the lids to kill all possible mold spores. Keeping lids scalding hot until used achieves the same results.

Q. What makes the undersides of metal lids turn dark?

A. The natural components in some foods may corrode the metal and cause brown or black deposits to form under the lid. They won't hurt you.

Q. Is it all right to let the jars cool in the water they were processed in?

A. No. The food will keep right on cooking in the water as it cools, giving you overcooked food.

Q. What's the purpose of exhausting the pressure canner?

A. If air is not forced out from inside the canner, the temperature inside will not correlate with the reading on the gauge. Food could easily be underprocessed if the inside temperature is lower than the temperature indicated on the gauge.

Q. Why must home-canned low-acid vegetables and non-acid foods (meats, poultry, and fish) be boiled before tasting?

A. Heating these foods to boiling and then hard simmer (205° to 210° F) for 15 minutes kills any spoilage organisms that might be present. A boiling temperature can also be reached if foods are baked, steamed, or fried for the suggested time.

Q. What if the jar seals and then later comes open?

A. The food has spoiled from underprocessing. Or food may have been left on jar rim, making an imperfect seal.

FRUIT PROBLEMS

Fruit floats to top of jar

1. Fruit syrup may have been too heavy.
2. Fruit may have been overripe.
3. Fruit was not packed tightly enough into jar.
4. Canning water was not hot at start of process.

Fruits darken at top of the jar

1. The cut, prepared fruit might have been exposed to the air too long before being canned, permitting oxidation or enzyme activity from the air.
2. Liquid in jar may not have covered food.
3. The correct canning time was not followed.
4. Too much head space was left or all air bubbles weren't removed.

Fruits darken after they are taken out of the jars

1. They weren't processed long enough after reaching hard simmer, so enzymes had gone to work.

Some fruits turn pink, red, blue, or purple when canned (pears, peaches, and apples especially)

1. When heated, chemical changes take place that alter the color of fruit. There is no way to avoid this.

JELLY PROBLEMS

Jelly is too soft

1. Too much juice in the mixture. Never increase recipe; stay with the 4 to 6 cups juice per recipe. Making too large a batch at once could also be the reason.
2. Mixture might have been too acid.
3. Mixture might have had too little sugar.

Jelly is syrupy

1. Too little pectin, acid, or sugar or too much sugar was used.

Jelly is too stiff

1. Too much pectin was used or the fruit was not ripe enough. Overcooking could also be the cause.

Jelly is cloudy

1. Jelly might have stood too long before being poured into glasses.
2. It might not have been strained well enough.
3. Jelly was poured too slowly into glasses.
4. Fruit was underripe.
5. Fruit was cooked too long.

PICKLING PROBLEMS

Hollow pickles

1. Cucumbers were poorly developed.
2. You waited too long between gathering cucumbers and using them.
3. Fermentation was too quick or temperature too high.
4. Brine wasn't strong or weak enough.

White sediment in jar bottom

1. If pickles are firm, it is only harmless yeast that has grown and settled.
2. If pickles are soft, this is a sign of spoilage and pickles shouldn't be eaten.
   Once a pickle becomes soft, it can't be made firm again. Microbial activity has caused spoilage.

Slippery or soft pickles

1. Not enough vinegar, brine, or salt was used.
2. The pickles weren't covered with liquid.
3. Scum wasn't removed from top and was allowed to drift through brine during fermentation.
4. Pickles weren't heated long enough.
5. The jars weren't sealed airtight.

Dark pickles

1. Minerals were present in the water, such as iron.
2. Iron, zinc, copper, or brass utensils were used.
3. Ground spices were used instead of whole spices; too much spice was used.
4. Pickles were overcooked.
5. Iodized salt was used.

VEGETABLE PROBLEMS

Liquid becomes cloudy

1. Spoilage may have set in and food shouldn't be eaten.

Green vegetables turn brown or lose bright color

1. Vegetables were too old for canning.
2. Vegetables were cooked too long.
3. Chlorophyll (responsible for the green color) was broken down by heat.

White sediment found in bottom of jars

1. Indicates starch from vegetables.
2. Hard minerals were present in water.
3. If water is murky, spoilage is indicated.

Freezing

For really quick, easy preserving, try freezing. You'll find foods taste and look much fresher than those preserved by any other method. And almost everything can be frozen. Whether you've just come home from the market with a good buy on ground beef or you want to preserve a surplus of corn from the garden, freezing is the answer.

Of course you'll need to have a freezer or access to a public locker. Owning a full freezer is a convenience and can actually pay for itself if you utilize it fully, keeping records of freezing dates and keeping items rotating from freezer to table.

What happens in freezing?

Freezing is a great way to preserve natural flavors in foods. The trick is to freeze food fast and keep it at 0° F or below for longer storage. When foods freeze, the organisms that cause spoilage and the enzymes that cause further ripening become inactive.

Food won't spoil as long as it stays solidly frozen at 0° F. Freezing doesn't actually destroy the bacteria or enzymes that cause spoilage. Bacteria and enzymes become active again when foods thaw. That's why defrosted foods often spoil more quickly than fresh. Botulism, however, does not occur in frozen foods. But freezing does cause some changes; the water content of the food forms ice crystals that can puncture cell walls. When the food thaws, natural juices run out and foods can become mushy. So avoid partial thawing and refreezing, for it increases cell damage and diminishes quality. The faster the freezing process, the smaller the ice crystals that form.

Even though foods kept at 15° or 25° F may seem as solidly frozen as foods at 10° F or below, they will have poorer quality when thawed. This is the disadvantage of using the small freezer compartment of a refrigerator. It doesn't stay cold enough, especially if there's lots of heavy traffic in and out of the refrigerator. It is wise to freeze only for short-term periods if your freezer temperature is above 10° F. Use a mercury-type freezer thermometer to determine whether your freezer can accommodate longer-term storage.

Use special freezing equipment

Determine the size of your freezer by the size of your family, your garden, or your need to have extra food on hand.

The way food is packaged has much to do with its quality when thawed. Air in the freezer container dries out frozen food and can cause color and flavor changes, sometimes referred to as *freezer burn*. The more airtight you make the container, the better quality will result.

Freezer instructions from the manufacturer will tell you how much food can be frozen at one time. Only the amount of unfrozen food that will freeze within 24 hours (about 2 to 3 pounds of food for each cubic foot of freezer space) should be put into the freezer at one time. Overloading cuts down the freezing rate and warms up the food already frozen. Foods lose quality and may spoil. Place unfrozen food packages next to freezing plates or coils, leaving a little space between packages so air can circulate. Packages can be stacked close together once frozen.

Canning jars are fine for freezing fruits and vegetables. Jars that are specifically designed for both canning and freezing have straight sides and wide mouths for easier removal of partially thawed foods.

Sturdy plastic boxes with tight-fitting lids also make good freezer containers.

Wax-lined cardboard boxes are very good. Plastic bags can be used to line these boxes for a really airtight seal.

Heavy plastic bags that close with rubber bands or wire twists can be used when it is important for the package to conform to the contour of the food, such as a whole chicken. Or the bags can be used inside the above-mentioned wax-lined cardboard boxes.

Freezer wraps, such as heavy aluminum foil, polyethylene sheets, clear plastic adhesive wrap, and any one of the coated, moisture-vaporproof, laminated freezer papers, are all fine for freezer use. They are particularly good for wrapping meat, fish, poultry, and whole vegetables, such as corn on the cob. (Use paper with wax on one side for very short storage only.)

Freezer tape, which has an adhesive that withstands low temperatures and moisture, is essential for labeling food. Identify the food and record the freezing date.

What about power failures?

Brownouts and blackouts are common occurrences today. If you are warned ahead of time of the failure, immediately turn your freezer to the coldest setting—the lower the temperature, the longer the food will stay frozen.

A fully packed freezer will stay colder longer than a partially filled one. A full freezer will usually keep food frozen for 2 days after a power failure, whereas a half-filled freezer may not keep food frozen more than 1 day.

Adding dry ice to the freezer will help keep the food frozen longer. Add it as soon as possible after the power goes off. A 50-pound block should keep the food temperature in a fully packed 20-cubic-foot freezer below freezing for 3 to 4 days. If the freezer is half filled or less, it will remain below freezing 2 to 3 days. As you work, be sure your room is well ventilated for air circulation. Don't put ice directly on the packages, and don't touch it with bare hands; wear heavy gloves. Only open the door to take food out or to add more dry ice.

Freezing Fresh Fruits

Happily, most fruits can be frozen. You need to consider which varieties freeze best before you start. The charts on pages 64-65 indicate which are best. In all cases, you'll want fruit to be ripe but firm and free from blemishes.

Prepare only the amount of fruit your freezer can freeze within 24 hours (check manufacturer's directions).

Is sugar necessary?

Some fruits can be packed in syrup, honey, or sugar; some need not be sweetened at all.

If you want to eat the fruit raw when partially thawed or if you want to use it in pies or other cooked dishes, the fruit can be frozen without a sweetener.

But you'll find that most fruits will taste better and retain their shapes best if some sugar or syrup is added.

You can add sugar directly to the fruit before freezing by gently mixing the two together with a spatula until fruit juices flow and sugar dissolves (usual proportions are about 1 part sugar to 4 to 5 parts fruit by weight).

Honey syrups are satisfactory only if your freezer stays at 0° F or below; at higher temperatures the honey may crystallize.

Prepare a packing syrup following the proportions given in the table below.

To pack fruits with syrup or sugar in wide-mouth containers, leave ½ inch head space at top for pints and 1 inch for quarts. With narrow-mouth containers, leave ¾ inch head space for pints and 1½ inches for quarts. Crumple a piece of waxed paper and place on top of fruit to hold it under the syrup or juice. With soft containers, such as plastic bags, exclude as much air as possible by submerging the bag of fruit in water all the way up to the opening. Then seal. When you seal the bags, make sure to leave the same head space as directed above for narrow-mouth containers. For other freezer containers, refer to the introductory information on page 61 and above.

agents are either added to the syrup in which the fruits are packed or dissolved in water and sprinkled over the fruits before packing. Drug stores sell ascorbic acid crystals or powder that can be used. Ascorbic acid tablets can also be used, but they tend to make syrups cloudy. The typical addition is ½ teaspoon pure ascorbic acid powder per quart of syrup. The tablets are more difficult to dissolve than the powder is (crush them first); a total of 1,500 milligrams ascorbic acid tablets is needed for each quart of syrup.

Commercial antidarkening agents, usually containing ascorbic and citric acids and often sugar, are also available. Follow the manufacturer's directions.

The chart occasionally calls for lemon juice for flavor; it is also used as an antidarkening agent. (If you use Meyer lemons, double the amount called for.) But note that the quantity needed to prevent darkening can make the fruit too tart.

SYRUP PROPORTIONS (Cups)	YIELD (Cups)
Light Syrup	
2 sugar, 4 water	5
1 honey, 1 sugar, 4 water	5½
1 honey, 3 water	4
Medium Syrup	
3 sugar, 4 water	5½
1 honey, 2 sugar, 4 water	6
2 honey, 2 water	4
Heavy Syrup	
4¾ sugar, 4 water	6½

Protecting fruit colors

Some fruits have a tendency to darken after they are cut; the fruit charts on pages 64-65 indicate which ones need to be treated. Antidarkening

Freezing Fresh Herbs

Freezing is a good way to preserve a few of the fresh, more tender herbs—basil, dill, chives, and tarragon. Simply wash, wipe dry, and freeze freshly picked herbs in small, airtight freezer bags, foil, or plastic wrap in amounts you might use at one time. Because frozen herbs will darken and become limp when thawed, add them directly from the freezer to the food you are cooking.

Freezing Guide for Fruits

Fruit and varieties	To yield 1 pint (pounds or pieces)	Preparation for freezing
Apples Golden Delicious, Winesap, Gravenstein, Jonathan, McIntosh, Newton Pippin	1¼ to 1½ lbs.	*To pack in syrup*, put ½ cup cold syrup (with antidarkening agent added) into each container. Pare and core apples and slice directly into syrup. Press down; add cold syrup to cover.
Apricots Blenheim (Royal), Tilton, Wenatchee Moorpark	1 to 1¼ lbs.	Peel by dipping in boiling water; plunge in cold water; then pull off skins. (Pare unevenly ripened fruit.) Cut in halves or quarters; remove pits. *To pack in syrup*, put ½ cup cold syrup (with antidarkening agent added) into each container; pack apricots. Add syrup to cover. *To pack in sugar*, sprinkle antidarkening solution over cut fruits; mix in ½ cup sugar per quart of fruit until sugar dissolves. Pack fruit and juice, pressing down until juice covers fruit.
Avocado	4 medium-sized Avocados	Peel fruit and remove pit. Mash and add 3 tablespoons lemon juice to each quart purée. Pack into containers.
Bananas		Not recommended for home freezing.
Berries (Strawberries: Lassen, Sequoia, Solana, Tioga, Wiltguard)	¾ to 1½ lbs.	Wash a few berries at a time; drain well. *Strawberries:* Slice or crush fruit and add ¾ to 1 cup sugar per quart of berries; let stand until dissolved; then pack. *Cranberries:* After washing, dry well. Spread single layer on trays, freeze uncovered, then pack. *Other berries:* Pack in containers; cover with cold syrup. Or gently mix sugar (¼ to ¾ cup per quart) with berries, and pack. Or freeze as for cranberries without sugar. Use within 3 months.
Cherries, Sweet Bing, Black Tartarian, Chinook, Lambert, Napoleon (Royal Ann)	1 to 1½ lbs.	Pit if desired (pits add flavor). *To pack in syrup*, put cherries in containers; cover with cold syrup (with antidarkening agent added). *To pack unsweetened*, leave stems on; dry after washing. Spread on trays in single layer; freeze uncovered; pack. Use within 3 months.
Coconut	1 to 1¼ whole Coconuts	Break husked coconut into halves by pounding shell around the center. Grate or grind meat. Pack into freezer containers, pressing coconut down. Seal and freeze. *To pack in syrup*, mix ½ cup sugar with 2 pounds (6 cups) grated coconut. Pack, pressing coconut down. Seal and freeze.
Dates	1¼ lbs.	Wash, drain well, pit if desired, pack, seal, and freeze without syrup.
Figs Black Mission, Black Spanish (Brown Turkey), Calimyrna, Celeste, Granata, Kadota, Laterula	¾ to 1¼ lbs.	Wash in ice water; remove stems; peel if desired (peel toughens). *To pack unsweetened*, pack in containers dry or cover with water (with antidarkening agent added). Use within 3 months. *To pack in syrup*, pack in containers and cover with cold syrup with antidarkening agent added.
Grapes Muscat, Thompson Seedless, Ribier, Perlette, Cardinal, Red Malaga, Tokay	2 lbs.	Wash, place in freezing containers (clusters or removed from stem). Make lemonade from frozen lemonade concentrate, decreasing water by 1 cup for each 6-ounce can. Pour over the grapes until they submerge. Cover and seal container; freeze. Or freeze washed grapes whole on cookie sheets. When frozen, place in freezer cartons or plastic bags and seal.
Grapefruit Marsh Seedless, Marsh Pink, Duncan, Seedling	2 lbs.	Wash, peel, cutting deep enough to remove white membrane under skin. Section; remove membranes and seeds. *To pack in syrup*, prepare a light syrup (may be part fruit juice). Seal and freeze. Or freeze without syrup.
Lemons and Limes		Squeeze them and freeze juice in ice cube trays. Store in plastic bags in freezer for later use.

Fruit and varieties	To yield 1 pint (pounds or pieces)	Preparation for freezing
Loquats	1½ to 2 lbs.	*To pack in syrup,* peel and cut fruit in halves; remove seeds. Cook until tender in syrup; chill. Pack in container and cover with cold syrup. Or purée (see below).
Mangoes	2 to 3 medium Mangoes	Wash, peel, cut off slice at stem end. Slice. Avoid meat near seed. *To pack in syrup,* put ½ cup cold, light syrup in each container; slice mangoes directly into cold syrup. Press slices down and add syrup to cover. Seal and freeze. *To pack in sugar,* place mango slices in a shallow bowl. Sprinkle with sugar, using 1 part sugar to 3 to 10 parts fruit by weight (½ cup sugar to 5 to 6 cups mango slices). Allow to stand a few minutes until sugar is dissolved. Mix gently. Pack, seal, and freeze.
Melons Cantaloupe, casaba, Crenshaw, honeydew, Persian, watermelon	1 to 1¼ lbs.	Peel and remove seeds. Cut in slices, cubes, or balls. *To pack in syrup,* put ½ cup cold syrup in each container. Cut fruit directly into syrup; cover with more syrup. For flavor add 1 teaspoon lemon juice to each cup syrup.
Nectarines Fire Globe, Freedom, Gold King, Gower, Late Grand, Le Grand, Marigold, Panamint, Rose, September Grand, Stanwick	1 to 1½ lbs.	Peel or pare as for Apricots (page 64). Cut in halves or slices and remove pits. *To pack in syrup,* put ½ cup cold syrup (with antidarkening agent added) in each container. Cut halves or slices directly into cold syrup. Press fruit down and cover with more syrup.
Oranges Do not use Navel.	3 to 4 medium Oranges	Wash, peel, cutting deep enough to remove white membrane under skin. Section; remove membrane and seeds. Freeze. *To pack in syrup,* cover with cold medium syrup. Liquid may be part juice from fruit. Seal and freeze.
Peaches Alawar, Elberta, Gold Medal, J.H. Hale, Late Crawford, Redglobe, Redhaven, Rio Oso Gem, Rochester, Slappy, Valient, Veteran	1 to 1½ lbs.	Peel or pare as for Apricots (page 64). Cut in halves or slices and remove pits. *To pack in syrup,* put ½ cup cold syrup (with antidarkening agent added) in each container. Cut halves or slices directly into cold syrup. Press fruit down and cover with more syrup.
Pears		Not recommended for home freezing.
Persimmons Freeze Fuyu, Hachiya as purée	1½ to 1¾ lbs.	*To pack whole,* dry fruit well after washing; remove stems. Freeze unwrapped on a tray; then wrap each persimmon individually in freezer foil or bags. To serve, hold frozen fruit under cold water, pull off skins, and eat while still frosty. Use within 3 months. *To freeze as purée,* see below.
Pineapple	⅘ lb.	Peel, remove core and eyes, cut in wedges, cubes, sticks, or thin slices, or crush. *To pack in cold syrup,* use a light syrup. Pack into containers and cover with syrup. Seal and freeze.
Plums and fresh prunes Duarte, El Dorado, Gaviota, Italian, Nubiana, President, Queen Ann, Santa Rosa, Standard, Stanley, Sugar, Wickson	1 to 1½ lbs.	Cut in halves and pit, or cut fruit away from pit in quarters. *To pack unsweetened,* leave plums whole; dry well after washing. Freeze uncovered on a tray, then pack in containers. Use cooked or in pies; use within 3 months. *To pack in syrup,* put ½ cup cold syrup (with antidarkening agent added) in each container. Pack fruit and add syrup to cover.
Rhubarb	⅔ to 1 lb.	Wash, trim, and cut rhubarb into pieces of desired length. Immerse in a quantity of boiling water; time 1 minute after boiling resumes; drain; cool quickly in ice water and drain well. *To pack unsweetened* (or sprinkled with sugar), pack into containers. *To pack in syrup,* pack blanched rhubarb tightly in containers; cover with cold syrup.
Tomatoes Freeze as purée, all types except beefsteak	1¼ to 2¼ lbs.	Freeze only as sauce, paste, or purée (see below).
Fruit purées and sauces All purées as indicated under *Preparation for freezing*		If necessary, cook or steam fruits until soft in a little water. Mash fruit, press through wire strainer, or whirl in a blender. Add sugar and/or lemon juice to taste. Heat to boiling; chill and pack.

No-Cook Freezer Jams

Some say there's all the difference in the world between frozen and canned jams. While frozen jams tend to be less thick than canned jams, they not only capture the fresh berry flavor and color but also take less time to make than the traditional boiled jam.

A word about pectin if you missed it before: two principal brands of powdered pectin are available. They vary in ounces, and one *cannot* be substituted for the other. Our first recipe requires the 2-ounce package; the fourth, the 1¾-ounce package.

When you make jams with two kinds of fruits, you can get some intriguing new flavors. Try one or all four recipes; you may become a convert to freezer jams.

Fresh Strawberry Jam

    4 cups hulled, well-crushed strawberries
       (approx. 8 cups fully ripe berries)
    1 package (2 oz.) powdered pectin
    1 cup light corn syrup
  5½ cups sugar
    4 tablespoons lemon juice

Turn crushed strawberries into a 2-quart kettle. Stirring vigorously, sift in powdered pectin slowly. Let stand 20 minutes, stirring strawberries occasionally so pectin thoroughly dissolves. Pour in corn syrup and mix well. Gradually stir in sugar.

When sugar is thoroughly dissolved, stir in lemon juice. Ladle jam into jars, cover, and then place in the freezer for 24 hours. (The jam won't freeze solid because of the sugar concentration.) If you want to keep jam longer than one month, store it in a freezer at a temperature of 10° F below zero to 20° above. Otherwise, you can store it in the refrigerator to use. Makes 4 pints.

Strawberry-Raspberry Jam

  2⅔ cups crushed strawberries (2 boxes)
  1⅓ cups crushed raspberries (1 box)
    1 package (2 oz.) powdered pectin
    1 cup light corn syrup
  5½ cups sugar
    2 tablespoons lemon juice

Place the 4 cups crushed berries in a 3-quart saucepan. Slowly sift in the powdered pectin, stirring constantly. Set aside for 30 minutes, stirring occasionally. Pour in corn syrup and mix well. Slowly stir in sugar and carefully heat mixture to 100° F (it should be lukewarm and no hotter). Ladle into half-pint-sized jars, cover securely, and freeze at least 24 hours or longer. Keep up to 6 months. Makes 8 half pints.

Strawberry-currant Jam. For this flavor combination, use 3¼ cups crushed strawberries and ¾ cup currant juice (see under Currant Jelly on page 29) for the 4 cups crushed berries; then follow directions above.

Freezer Peach Jam

    2 cups peeled, thinly sliced peaches
    3 tablespoons lemon juice
    4 cups sugar
    1 package (1¾ oz.) powdered pectin
    1 cup water

In a heatproof bowl, combine the peaches and lemon juice, using a fork or pastry blender to crush fruit. Stir in the sugar and let stand about 20 minutes, stirring occasionally. In a saucepan, combine the pectin and water. Bring to a boil and boil for 1 minute, stirring constantly.

Pour hot pectin mixture into the peaches; stir for 2 minutes. Pour into clean jars or small freezer containers, covering with clean lids or with foil.

Let stand at room temperature for about 1 hour or until fruit is set.

The jam keeps well in the refrigerator for several weeks. Freeze for longer storage; then transfer to the refrigerator as needed. Makes 4 to 5 cups.

If You Have Too Many Tomatoes...

The tomato crop—even from one home grown plant—can be a bit overwhelming. And when it comes time to harvest tomatoes, you may find your supply will perish faster than you can consume it. Besides canning tomatoes, one solution is to turn some of them into a sauce that you can freeze for use throughout the year.

This well-seasoned, basic sauce uses lots of medium-sized tomatoes. And it can be served in various ways. See the serving suggestions that follow the recipe; then consider trying flavor combinations of your own.

Basic Fresh Tomato Sauce

2 **medium-sized onions, finely chopped**
4 **cloves garlic, minced or mashed**
⅓ **cup olive oil or salad oil**
5 **pounds (about 12 medium-sized) firm-ripe tomatoes**
  Boiling water
½ **cup minced green onion (including part of the green tops)**
1 **green pepper, seeded and chopped**
1½ **teaspoons salt**
¾ **teaspoon pepper**
¼ **teaspoon anise seed, crushed**
1 **tablespoon oregano leaves**
¾ **teaspoon rosemary leaves**
1 **teaspoon paprika**
  About 1¾ cups dry red wine

In a Dutch oven or large frying pan, cook onions and garlic in olive oil over medium heat until golden (about 15 minutes); stir occasionally.

Meanwhile, immerse tomatoes, a few at a time, in boiling water to cover for 1 minute; then lift out and plunge into cold water. Pull off and discard skin. Cut tomatoes into eighths and add to cooked onions, along with the green onion, green

pepper, salt, pepper, anise seed, oregano, rosemary, paprika, and the 1¾ cups dry red wine. Bring mixture to boiling, stirring with a heavy wooden spoon to break up tomatoes. Cover, reduce heat, and simmer for 1 hour. Remove cover and boil until reduced to 8 cups.

You can use the sauce while hot, let it cool and refrigerate for 3 days, or freeze up to 4 months. If you freeze the sauce, divide it into 1, 2, or 4-cup sized portions to use according to the suggestions below.

To reheat the sauce (if frozen, let it thaw first), bring mixture to simmering over low heat, stirring occasionally. If sauce appears dry, blend in 2 to 4 tablespoons water or dry red wine. Makes about 2 quarts.

Serving the Tomato Sauce

With pasta. Cook about 6 to 8 ounces spaghetti or other pasta according to package directions; then drain well. Pour onto a platter and mix with about 4 cups heated Basic Fresh Tomato Sauce; sprinkle with chopped parsley. Accompany with shredded Parmesan cheese. Makes 6 to 8 first-course servings.

With beef or shellfish. Spoon heated Basic Fresh Tomato Sauce onto individual servings of broiled beef steaks or ground beef patties or servings of hot cooked scallops, cold crab, or boiled or broiled shelled and deveined shrimp. Allow about 2 cups sauce for 4 to 5 servings.

With vegetables. Heat 1 cup Basic Fresh Tomato Sauce with 1 tablespoon chopped parsley. Stir it into 1 pound hot cooked whole green beans or 1¼ pounds hot, cooked sliced zucchini. Sprinkle with 3 tablespoons toasted pine nuts (stir nuts in a small, dry frying pan over medium heat just until golden). Makes 4 servings.

Freezing Fresh Vegetables

Vegetable gardens are springing up on almost any postage-stamp-size plot available these days, and are also being cultivated. If you're one of those who has more fresh vegetables than you can use and have given all away you can—consider freezing part of the crop for later use.

Successful home freezing depends on absolutely fresh vegetables. Here the home gardener has a distinct advantage: he can pick vegetables at the peak of maturity and freeze them without delay. (To determine the best time to pick your crop, see the special feature, pages 72–73.)

To freeze food at home successfully and be able to keep it frozen for more than just a couple of weeks or so, you need a freezer that stays at 0° F or lower without dramatically fluctuating. Vegetables will freeze quickly at this temperature with minimum texture deterioration.

How to prepare vegetables for freezing

Vegetables should be fully ripened but still young and as freshly picked as possible. Wash them well in cold water and prepare them as directed in the charts on pages 70–71. Prepare at one time only the amount your freezer can freeze within 24 hours (see manufacturer's instruction booklet). Get freezer containers out (see pages 61–62), washed and ready to use.

Most vegetables need to be heated before they are packed by a process called *blanching* (directions follow). This helps preserve color, flavor, texture, and nutritive value. Follow the blanching times given on the chart for each vegetable. Use the shorter amount of time for small, young vegetables; apply the longer times to more mature vegetables or those cut in larger pieces. Increase blanching time by one minute if you live 5,000 feet or more above sea level.

Some vegetables require treatment to prevent darkening, just as fruits do; the charts on pages 70–71 specify which ones. Since you don't freeze vegetables with liquid or syrup as you do fruits, the antidarkening agent is added to the blanching water. Citric acid (available in drugstores) or lemon juice is usually used with vegetables. The amounts are specified on the charts; double the amount of lemon juice if you use Meyer lemons.

To blanch vegetables, place no more than 2 pounds at a time in a wire basket, metal colander, or cheesecloth bag. Immerse in a large pan of rapidly boiling water. When boiling resumes, cover and start counting blanching time (see charts on pages 70–71). If it takes more than two minutes to resume boiling, use fewer vegetables the next time.

Immediately chill blanched vegetables by plunging the basket into ice water or under cold running water until completely cold.

How to package vegetables for freezing

Pack vegetables in freezer containers. Loose vegetables, such as cut green beans and mushrooms, are usually packed in plastic freezer bags placed in cardboard freezer cartons; the cartons make stacking easier and protect bags from tearing. Wrap corn on the cob in heavy-duty freezer foil or freezer wraps. Rigid containers, such as plastic boxes with tight-fitting lids or canning jars, are convenient for packing solid vegetables, such as cooked winter squash.

In any container, it's important to exclude as much air as possible. With plastic bags, submerge all but the bag opening in water to force out air. Foods expand as they freeze, so leave a head space of ½ inch for soft containers and 1 inch for rigid containers or solid-pack vegetables. Seal as directed for the type of container used—twist wire ties on plastic bags; attach lids to plastic freezer boxes; screw ring bands down over lids on canning jars. Label and freeze immediately.

Vegetable Purées

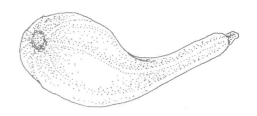

Another easy way to preserve the summer goodness of squash and cucumbers is to purée them. Perhaps the most remarkable attribute of vegetable purées is the way they retain fresh garden flavors month after month in the freezer. Combining them with other flavorings, such as onion, green pepper, and herbs, makes them especially convenient for making hot or cold vegetable soups, simple vegetable casseroles, or other dishes you may devise on your own.

Frozen Summer Squash Purée

6 pounds summer squash (crookneck, patty-
    pan, or zucchini)
2 green peppers
3 large onions, thinly sliced
6 tablespoons butter or margarine
¼ cup water
3 cloves garlic
2¼ teaspoons salt
½ teaspoon pepper
1 cup lightly packed parsley sprigs
1 cup lightly packed fresh basil leaves or ¼
    cup lightly packed fresh tarragon leaves
    (optional)

Scrub well and remove stem and blossom ends from squash. Cut into thin slices (you should have 5 quarts). Remove seeds from peppers and cut into thin slices.

In an 8-quart or larger pan over medium heat, melt the butter. Put in onions and cook, stirring, until soft (about 10 minutes). Add the water and stir in the squash, green peppers, garlic, salt, and pepper. Cover and cook for 3 minutes; then turn heat to medium-high. Continue cooking, covered (remove cover often to stir and turn the mixture), until squash is very tender (12 to 15 minutes).

Remove from heat; stir in the parsley. If desired, add the basil or tarragon.

To prepare purée, whirl about ½ cup of the vegetables with pan juices in a blender container until smooth. Then add more vegetables and juices (about ½ cup at a time) until there are about 3 cups of purée in the container; pour this into a large bowl. Repeat until all vegetables are puréed. Cool to room temperature.

Pack in freezer containers, such as plastic boxes with tight-fitting lids, canning jars, or plastic freezer bags placed in cardboard freezer cartons. If you use tall, straight, or slightly flared containers or bags, leave ½ inch head space for pints and 1 inch for quarts. For low, broad containers, allow ¼ inch head space for pints and ½ inch for quarts. Seal as directed for the type of container used. Label and freeze at once. Fills about 6 pint-sized containers.

Frozen Cucumber Purée

7½ pounds cucumbers
6 tablespoons butter or margarine
3 large onions, thinly sliced
¼ cup water
2¼ teaspoons salt
½ teaspoon pepper
1 cup lightly packed parsley sprigs

Peel the cucumbers and cut into thin slices (you should have 5 quarts). Melt the butter in an 8-quart or larger pan over medium heat. Put in the onions and cook, stirring, until they are soft (about 10 minutes). Add the water, stir in the cucumbers, salt, and pepper. Cover and cook for about 5 minutes or until liquid forms in the pan and comes to boiling. Increase heat to medium-high and continue cooking, uncovered, stirring often, until cucumber is limp (10 to 15 minutes).

Remove from heat and stir in the parsley. Prepare purée and pack it in containers in the same way you pack Frozen Summer Squash Purée (see above). Fills about 6 pint-sized containers.

Summer squash casserole. In a bowl, beat 2 eggs lightly with a fork. Stir in contents of 1 pint-sized container of summer squash purée (thawed). Pour into a greased, shallow baking dish (3 or 4-cup capacity). Sprinkle with ½ cup freshly shredded Parmesan cheese. Set casserole inside a larger pan filled about ½ inch deep with hottest tap water. Bake in a 350° oven until set (30 to 35 minutes). You may sprinkle the top when you serve it with about ⅓ cup coarsely chopped, toasted almonds. Serves 4.

Cucumber Casserole. Prepare same as squash casserole except use 3 eggs.

Freezing Guide for Vegetables

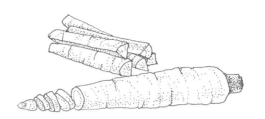

Vegetables for freezing	To yield 1 pint (pounds or pieces)	Preparation for freezing
Artichokes	20 to 25 1¼-inch trimmed artichokes	*For whole medium-sized artichokes,* pull off coarse outer bracts; cut 1 inch off tops; trim off thorny tips; trim stems. Wash. Blanch 10 minutes (add 3 teaspoons citric acid or ½ cup lemon juice to 2 quarts water). Chill. Pack in freezer plastic bags. *For artichoke hearts,* cut off top third of small artichokes; trim all but ½ inch of stems. Pull off all bracts down to edible pale leaves. Blanch 3 to 5 minutes, adding citric acid or lemon juice as for whole artichokes (see above).
Asparagus	1 to 1½ lbs.	Cut off tough ends of stalks. Sort for even sizes. Wash. blanch 2 to 4 minutes. Chill. Pack in freezer plastic bags.
Beans; string, wax, and Italian	⅔ to 1 lb.	Wash and snap off ends. Cut in 1-inch pieces or cut lengthwise. Blanch 2 to 3 minutes. Chill. Pack in freezer plastic bags.
Beans, Lima	2 to 2½ lbs.	Shell and wash beans; sort for size. Blanch 2 to 4 minutes.
Beets	1¼ to 1½ lbs.	Remove tops. Wash and peel. Leave whole if small, or slice or dice. Blanch 3 to 5 minutes. Cook mature beets in water until tender. Chill. Pack in freezer plastic bags.
Broccoli	1 lb.	Trim outer leaves and wash carefully. Split large stalks to ½-inch thickness. Sort for size. Blanch 3 to 4 minutes. Chill. Pack in freezer plastic bags.
Brussels Sprouts	1 lb.	Trim, remove outer leaves, and wash. Sort for size; blanch 3 to 5 minutes. Chill. Pack in freezer plastic bags.
Cabbage	1 to 1½ lbs.	Discard outside and defective leaves. Cut heads into convenient-sized pieces. Blanch 3 to 4 minutes, depending on size. Drain, chill, pack, and freeze.
Carrots	1¼ to 1½ lbs.	Remove tops. Wash and scrape or peel. Use small, tender carrots whole; dice or slice others into ½-inch pieces. Blanch 2 minutes for slices; 5 minutes for whole. Chill. Pack in freezer plastic bags.
Cauliflower	1¼ lbs.	Break into 1-inch pieces. Wash well. Blanch 3 minutes (add 1 tablespoon vinegar to 1 gallon blanching water). Chill. Pack in freezer plastic bags.
Celery	1 lb.	Trim crisp stalks. Wash thoroughly and cut into 1-inch lengths. Blanch 3 minutes; cool in ice water and drain. Pack, seal, and freeze.
Chayote	1½ to 2 lbs.	Wash, remove stem and blossom ends. Do not peel. Dice. Blanch 2 minutes, cool in ice water; drain. Pack, seal, and freeze.
Chinese edible pod peas	⅔ to 1 lb.	Remove stem and blossom ends and any string. Blanch for 1½ minutes. Chill. Pack in freezer plastic bags.
Corn	2 to 2½ lbs. (6 to 8 ears)	Husk, remove silk, and wash. Sort for size. *For kernels,* blanch whole ears 4 minutes; cool quickly; cut kernels from the cob. Chill. Pack in freezer plastic bags. *For corn on cob,* pierce cob lengthwise with a sharp instrument; blanch 3 to 4 minutes; chill very thoroughly. Pack in containers, plastic bags, freezer wrap, or heavy-duty freezer foil.
Eggplant	1 to 1½ lbs.	Wash, peel, and cut in ½-inch-wide fingers or dice. Blanch 2 to 4 minutes according to size. After cooling, prevent darkening by dipping in solution of 1 tablespoon citric acid or ½ cup lemon juice in 5 cups water. Drain well. Pack in freezer plastic bags.

Vegetables for freezing	To yield 1 pint (pounds or pieces)	Preparation for freezing
Ginger Root	1 whole piece	Wash well and dry. Do not blanch. Wrap whole, uncut, in moisture-vapor-resistant material. Seal and freeze. *To use,* grate or slice unthawed root. Return unused portion to freezer.
Greens		(see under Spinach, below)
Kohlrabi	1¼ to 1½ lbs.	Use firm, small roots 2 to 3 inches in diameter. Cut off and discard tops. Wash, peel, and dice. Blanch 1½ minutes. Cool quickly, drain, pack, seal, and freeze.
Mushrooms	1 to 2 lbs.	Wash thoroughly. Trim stem. Leave whole or slice. Blanch 2 to 4 minutes according to size (add 1 tablespoon lemon juice to 1 quart blanching water). Or sauté in butter until tender. Chill. Pack in freezer plastic bags.
Okra	1 to 1½ lbs.	Wash, cut off stems, but don't open seed cells. Blanch small pods 3 minutes; large pods 4 minutes. Cool in ice water; drain. Leave whole or slice crosswise. Pack, seal, and freeze.
Onions (yellow or white)	1 to 3 whole	Peel, chop, don't blanch. Freeze in small freezer bags to have on hand. Use in two months.
Parsnips	1¼ to 1½ lbs.	Cut off tops, wash thoroughly in cold running water. Peel. Cut in ½-inch cubes or slices. Blanch 2 minutes. Cool in ice water 5 minutes; drain. Pack, seal, and freeze.
Peas	2 to 3 lbs.	Shell peas, wash. Blanch 1½ minutes. Pack in freezer plastic bags.
Peppers (red or green bell)	1 to 3 lbs.	Wash, remove stem and seeds. Cut in halves or slices. Do not blanch. Pack in small containers for convenience.
Potatoes, new	2 to 4 lbs.	Cook until barely tender. Chill. Pack in freezer plastic bags. Thaw in bags when ready to use.
Baked and stuffed		Bake and stuff as usual; cool, wrap individually in foil, and freeze. Then place in freezer plastic bags or heavy-duty freezer foil, seal, and freeze.
Rutabaga	1¼ to 1½ lbs.	Cut off tops, peel, and dice. Blanch 1 minute. Cool quickly, drain, pack, seal, and freeze.
Spinach and other greens	1 to 1½ lbs.	Wash to clean off sand and grit; cut off heavy stems. Blanch leaves 1½ minutes, stirring well. Chill and drain. Pack in freezer plastic bags.
Squash (summer varieties); Crookneck, patty pan, zucchini	1 to 1¼ lbs.	Wash and cut off stem ends. Cut in ½-inch slices. Blanch 3 minutes. Chill. Pack in containers.
Squash (winter varieties); Banana, butternut, Hubbard, pumpkin	1 to 1½ lbs.	Wash and peel. Cut open and remove seed; cut into chunks. Cook until soft in small amount of water, then mash; cool. Pack in rigid containers.
Tomatoes		(See under Guide to Freezing Fruit chart, page 65.)
Water Chestnuts		Unused portions of canned water chestnuts may be frozen.

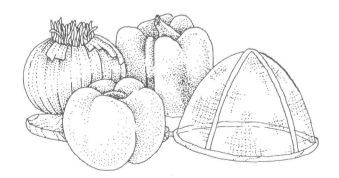

Home Harvesting... When to Pick, Which to Pick

Growing your own vegetables gives you the chance to enjoy them at their best. But figuring out exactly when they reach that plump, sweet stage is trickier than veteran vegetable growers often make it seem.

Harvesting too soon keeps the crops from reaching full size and, often, full flavor. *Harvesting too late* may increase size, but it's at the expense of flavor and tenderness; and a vegetable left on the plant too long drains energy and slows further production.

In August, when most crops grow rapidly, it's a good idea to check their progress every day. Hunt thoroughly for ripe or aging vegetables and pick right away. If you go away during harvest time, have someone come in to pick vegetables as they ripen.

In addition to the signs of ripeness given in the following list, there's a simple test that works for many vegetables: Pick a few samples and taste for sweetness and crispness.

Artichokes. Where artichokes are grown commercially, they yield over a long period. Elsewhere, spring harvest period is short and plants need extra care. Cut flower buds (the artichokes) when they are 2 to 4 inches in diameter and while scales or bracts are still tight. Cut with 1½ inches of stalk.

Asparagus. This perennial crop should grow undisturbed the first season after planting. During the second spring, cut spears for 4 to 6 weeks; then permit foliage to grow to strengthen the root system for next year's crop. In subsequent springs, cut for 8 to 10 weeks. Discontinue cutting when thin spears begin to appear; these show that root strength is declining.

Cut spears at ground level or 1½ inches below; don't cut deeply enough to injure root crown. Use a sharp knife or (preferably) an asparagus knife with a V-shaped notch for a cutting edge.

Beans (green or wax). Look for young, tender, long, sleek pods with beans just starting to bulge sides. Test by breaking in half; beans that will taste best snap with a pop, show no or few fibers. Aging pods turn yellow, leathery, stringy, streaked, with mealy beans inside.

Beets. The smaller the better, once beety flavor develops; best when 1 to 2 inches in diameter. You can eat tops and roots of small beets you thin out. Old beets bump out of the ground, split sides, taste woody. Pickle surplus rather than leave them in the ground. To harvest greens, cut when foliage is dark, before leaves turn yellow.

Broccoli. Cut while clustered flower heads are firm and green. Take heads with leaves and 5 or 6 inches of stem (also edible). Don't damage short side branches; they will produce smaller heads if left to grow.

Brussels sprouts. Twist or snap off sprouts when they are firm and still deep green (usually about the time lowest big leaves start to yellow). Harvest lowest sprouts first. Upper ones will continue to enlarge to harvesting size.

Cabbage. Harvest when heads are firm to the touch. Cut off head and a few wrapper leaves with a sharp knife.

Carrots. Young ones are sweetest and most tender; start pulling at finger size or when you need to thin crowded plants. Except for biggest varieties, carrots turn woody when over 1½ inches in diameter. In tight soil, water first; then carefully tug and tease carrots to avoid breaking them or injuring neighboring ones.

Cauliflower. As soon as blossom heads (farmers call them curds) begin to form, tie up outer leaves over them to shade them from the sun. This blanching process gives a white curd. Inspect from time to time and cut off curd before the flower sections begin to separate.

Corn. Good timing is critical because sugar in kernels turns to starch as soon as ear is picked or reaches a certain age—and then it's no better than store-bought. Perfectionists say to start the water boiling and then go out and pick.

As first sign of coming ripeness, green silks wither to brown; feel for plump kernels through husk. To make sure corn's ripe, peel back husk at top and pierce a kernel with thumbnail. Milky juice spurts out if ear is just right. Clear juice means wait a day or two. Insides like toothpaste mean you've missed your chances for perfection on that ear.

Cucumber. With most varieties, pick for sweet pickles when 2 or 3 inches long, for dills when 5 or 6 inches, for slicing when 6 or 8 inches. Lemon cucumber should measure no wider than 3 inches. Japanese and Armenian cucumbers retain quality even up to 20 inches long. Cut or snap off, leaving short stem.

Eggplant. It's most tender and you hardly notice small seeds if you pick when glossy, dark purple, and 4 to 6 inches long (it can grow much larger). Pick long, slender Japanese eggplant when finger size to hot-dog size; one plant will bear dozens if you keep them picked.

Kohlrabi. Pull when bulbs are 2 to 2½ inches in diameter. Cut off taproot. Use bulb and leaves.

Leek. For long, white leeks, prepare by blanching—either in a trench, by shading with waterproof paper cylinders, or by drawing up soil around the plants. Use when blanched (white) portion is 1 to 1½ inches thick.

Lettuce. Hot weather quickly forces seed production and bitter flavor. For heading lettuce such as iceberg, harvest when center feels firm. For leaf (loose-head) lettuce, cut or pull outer leaves when you can use them; inner leaves grow quickly to eating size.

Lima beans. Pods should be green, with swellings to show the beans inside. Open a pod or two; beans should be plump but still green or gray green (not white). Pick often to prolong picking season.

Melons. These are tricky. Smell is as good a clue as any (except for watermelon); sniff for characteristic aroma at blossom end.

Cantaloupe. Nudge gently; if it slips from the stem, it's ready. Another sign; Netting on skin becomes prominent.

Casaba. Leave on the vine until blossom end softens and rind turns yellow.

Crenshaw. It's ripe (and highly perishable) when dark green skin develops yellow streaks.

Honeydew. Pick when blossom end softens and white skin turns cream color.

Watermelon. Think about harvesting when curly tendril on vine next to fruit stem withers. Further confirmation: Where rind touches ground it turns from white to light yellow. Folk method of rapping on melon works if you have a good ear: ripe melon goes "pong" instead of "ping."

Onions and garlic. You can use some onions green and leave the rest to grow up. Pull green onions when stalk is thick as a pencil; even young ones have good flavor. Harvest dry onions and garlic when tops dry up and fall over. (You can harvest sooner but bulbs won't store well.) Loosen ground with spade or fork, then tug them out. Let bulbs dry on top of ground for a few days. Remove tops before storing.

Parsnips. Use as soon as roots are large enough to cook. Or, if you wish, leave roots in ground until needed. They will tolerate almost any cold, but, of course, you can't dig them if the ground is frozen solid. Use before spring regrowth.

Peas. As with string beans, a simple test is to pick and taste a few. Peas should be formed inside the pods but should be tender and deep green. Smaller ones are tastier than the bigger ones. Pick frequently to prolong production.

Sugar or snow peas with edible pods should be picked as soon as peas are perceptible inside the pods.

Peppers. Pick sweet green peppers (bell peppers) anytime after they reach worthwhile size. If left to mature, late in the season they turn bright red, mellow, and sweet. Pick hot peppers when they have reached full size and desired color—red, yellow, or green.

Potatoes. Start digging new potatoes when plants bloom; use right away or keep in refrigerator. Harvest old potatoes when tops die back; slip spade or fork deep under clump and lift to surface. Leave in sun only long enough for soil to dry; shake off soil. Store in cool, dark, dry place.

Spinach. Cut or pinch off outer leaves to eat as they reach full size. Let small inner ones grow to prolong harvest.

Squash. Zucchini and other long green summer squashes are most tender between 5 and 8 inches long (up to 10 inches for some varieties). At ultimate size of 2 feet and more, they become fibrous, seedy, and tough skinned. Bake overgrown squash if skin is still tender enough for you to pierce it with light push of thumbnail. Blooms can turn into edible-sized squash in a couple of nights; search plants every other day.

Yellow crookneck varieties taste best when 4 to 7 inches long. Pick when pale yellow rather than golden, before skin hardens.

Harvest scalloped squash (pattypan) when it's grayish or greenish white, before it turns ivory white. It's best while small, even silver-dollar size.

Winter squash (acorn, Hubbard, spaghetti) and pumpkins develop hard shells and can store until spring if allowed to mature. Pick after vine dries up. Leave on the ground until frost, if you want, but in hot valleys harvest or protect from sunburn when vine foliage withers away. Cut with 2 or 3-inch stems on. Store in dry place between 45° and 55°F.

Tomatoes. Wait for deep red color (except for yellow and orange varieties) and firm flesh. To beat frosts at end of season, pick all fruit on vine and let green ones ripen in a warm place.

Turnips and rutabagas. Pull young plants with tiny roots to thin rows and give growing room to the remaining plants. Eat thinnings, tops and all. At 2-inch diameters, roots are tastiest, and tops are still good as greens. At 3 inches and above, roots are still good and store a little better. Late-planted rutabagas can stay in the ground until needed.

Freezing Meat, Poultry, & Seafood

Having meat, poultry, or seafood on hand in your freezer can be a ready convenience, can save you many trips to the grocery store, and can be a boost to your food budget. Keep an eye out for whole bargain chicken or sides of beef, offered at lower prices. A freezer allows you to take advantage of these specials.

You can buy whole carcasses, sides, or quarters of meat as wholesale cuts, or as retail cuts when they are a bargain at your supermarket.

Your meat is guaranteed *wholesome* if it bears the round, purple USDA inspection stamp. Quality is insured with a shield-shaped USDA grade mark. It indicates tenderness, juiciness, and flavor. Do not confuse the two.

When you buy a whole carcass or side (half a carcass) of *beef*, you get a wide range of cuts—some of which you may not want or wouldn't ordinarily have purchased. Or you may want to buy just the cuts you're certain you'll use from either wholesale or retail sources. When you buy the whole or half carcass, you are paying for the untrimmed weight. So figure you can lose about 25 percent of the poundage you purchase. (A rule of thumb is 25 percent waste, 25 percent ground beef and stew meat, 25 percent steaks, and 25 percent roasts.) A hindquarter of beef will yield more steaks and roasts but will cost more per pound than a forequarter; but the yield of usable lean meat is greater than that from the forequarter.

Buying *lamb* is easier than buying beef because the quality of lamb is less variable. "Lamb" is produced from animals less than one year old.

The United States Department of Agriculture (USDA) grades pork as either acceptable or unacceptable. All retail markets only handle acceptable grades. You will want to buy a whole, acceptable pork carcass from an establishment that can render the lard and cure the bacon, hams, and other cuts that you may not want to use fresh. If you can't have this done, you should probably just buy wholesale cuts of fresh pork and hams. Then look for cuts with small amounts of fat over the outside, and firm, grayish pink meat.

The amount of meat you buy for the freezer will depend on how much freezer space you have, how much your family will need, how much your budget allows, and how much meat your freezer freezes at one time (see manufacturer's booklet).

For large meat purchases, it's usually best to have freezing done by a commercial meat market, since all the meat needs to be frozen at once. Slower freezing (freezing batches at home) causes more cells to rupture because of formation of large ice crystals, so that more meat juices are lost when the meat is thawed.

Properly wrapped meat cuts, stored at 0° F or lower, will keep their quality for a long time. Meat should be quickly frozen at 10° F or lower, with space left for air circulation between packages.

Use moisture-vaporproof wrap, such as heavy aluminum foil, heavily waxed freezer paper, or specially laminated paper. Wrap meat closely, eliminating all air, if possible. Place double thickness of waxed paper between chops and steaks so they won't stick. Seal packages well and label with the date.

Although it's safe to refreeze meat that has been thawed in the refrigerator, you can expect a loss of quality.

Suggested storage time for meat at 0° F.

Beef	
Ground	3-4 months
Pieces or cubes	6-8 months
Roasts, steaks	8-12 months
Lamb	
Ground	3-4 months
Roasts, chops	8-12 months
Pork	
Ground sausage	1-3 months
Roasts, chops	6-8 months
Smoked pork or ham	1-3 months

Preparing meat for the freezer

You can lay to rest two common misconceptions about freezing: it neither tenderizes nor sterilizes meat. What it does do is to inactivate most enzymes and kill some of the bacteria and molds normally present in meat. Start by making sure all utensils and cutting boards are spotlessly clean before you begin cutting the meat to freeze.

First chill the carcass; then cut it into pieces for intended use (roasts, chops, and so forth) if you are doing the cutting yourself. To save freezer space, trim off excess fat before wrapping, and bone pieces with a high percentage of bone.

Wrap in moisture-vapor-resistant paper, plastic, or freezer foil. Press wrapping firmly against meat, forcing out all air pockets. You can either drugstore wrap or butcher wrap the meat.

To drugstore wrap, place meat in center of paper, using enough paper so both edges can fold down against meat two or three times. Bring the two edges of paper together above the meat and make a folding crease. Fold down in ½-inch to 1-inch folds until the paper is tight against meat. Press out as much air as possible at each end. Fold ends down and tightly back against package (like gift wrapping). Secure with freezer tape or string.

To butcher wrap, place meat close to one corner of the paper. Fold a corner against the meat and the side of paper over the meat. Roll the package over and over until all paper is used. Secure with freezer tape or string. Separate each layer of meat with two pieces of moistureproof paper. Label, giving the cut of meat, weight or number of servings, and date. Freeze at 0° F.

Preparing poultry for freezing

Chickens, ducks, geese, and turkeys can be frozen whole, halved, quartered, or cut up. Never stuff poultry before freezing because the stuffing takes so long to cool inside the bird during freezing and to thaw and reheat during roasting, that food spoilage and bacteria growth can take place, causing food poisoning.

To freeze whole, wrap and freeze giblets separately, for they develop off-flavors in about 3 months. If you use the poultry within 3 months, you can wrap the giblets in freezer wrap and place them in the body cavity.

Tie leg ends of the cleaned bird together. Press the wings close to the body.

Place the bird in the center of the wrapping sheet, bring long sides over the bird, and fold together about 1 inch of edges. Fold again to bring the sheets tight and flat on top of the bird. Press wrapping close to the bird to force air out. At each end, fold corners toward each other. Fold ends upward and over until the package is tight. You can package poultry in plastic bags, pressing out as much air as possible before fastening bags. (Dip the filled bag in ice water, holding the open end above the water. Press the bag against the poultry and upward, expelling air.

To freeze half birds, package halves together or separately. If together, place a double piece of wrapping paper between them.

To freeze cut-up birds, wash the pieces in cold water and dry. Separate meaty pieces from bony ones (use bony pieces in soup). Place meaty pieces close together in a freezer bag or carton, or wrap in freezer paper. Separate each piece of poultry with a piece of freezer paper to hasten thawing. (Darkening near the leg bones is caused by seepage of blood from the bone marrow during freezing, thawing, and cooking—the quality of flesh isn't affected.)

Store chicken and turkey 6–12 months.

Freezing seafood

Fish must be kept cold after being caught, quickly cleaned, and frozen to keep well. Freeze whole small fish; cut large fish into steaks, fillets, or boned strips. To prevent darkening and rancidity of fatty fish, such as tuna and salmon, dip in ascorbic acid solution (2 tablespoons ascorbic acid to 1 quart water) for 20 seconds. Wrap in moisture-vaporproof paper in meal-size packages, separating pieces with two pieces of freezing paper or foil. Freeze quickly and store at 0° F.

Shellfish can be frozen easily. For *shrimp,* remove heads but don't shell. Wash in a solution of 1 teaspoon salt to 1 quart water. Drain, package in freezer containers, seal, and freeze at 0° F.

For *clams* and *oysters,* shuck or open, collecting meat in a colander to drain. Wash thoroughly and quickly in solution of 1 tablespoon salt to 1 quart water; drain. Package shellfish in canning jars, sturdy plastic boxes, or wax-lined cardboard boxes (see pages 61–62); cover with reserved juices, leaving ½ inch head space. Seal and freeze at 0° F.

For *crab,* break off claws and legs. Remove back shell, gills, crab butter, and other viscera. Wash thoroughly. Prepare as soon as caught. Steam 15 to 20 minutes in order to preserve color and flavor. Cool slightly. Then pick meat from body and legs while warm, keeping meats separate. Tightly package in glass jars or freezer containers (see pages 61–62), removing as much air as possible to prevent ice crystals from forming; these cause meat to toughen. If stored for more than 4 months, cover with a solution of 3 tablespoons salt mixed with 1 gallon water. Leave ½ inch head space. Seal and freeze at 0° F. To freeze crab in the shell, carefully package each one immediately in an airtight wrapper, preferably in an ice-salt mixture (8 parts crushed ice to 1 part salt). Although discoloration will take place, the meat will still have a good flavor.

Store fatty fish, such as salmon and tuna, 1–3 months; lean fish, such as haddock and cod, 4–6 months.

Store crab and lobster 1–2 months; oysters 1–3 months; clams and scallops 3–4 months; shrimp 4–6 months.

Freezing Guide for Prepared Foods

Food	Preparation/Packaging	To Serve	Storage Time
Appetizers, Hors d'Oeuvres (Also see Sandwiches, Closed, page 81)	Prepare as usual: Small, open-faced sandwiches Rolled canapes Puff shells Stuffed nuts and olives Bacon-wrapped tidbits Cheese rolls Dips and spreads of cheese, deviled ham, fish, avocado, and egg yolk mixtures Before packaging, spread appetizers in single layers on metal pans and freeze. Package toast or crisp base appetizers separately from other appetizers. Use shallow containers which hold not more than 2 to 3 layers. Separate layers with pieces of moisture-resistant paper. Overwrap entire container with moisture-vapor-resistant paper.	Toast and crisp base appetizers: Thaw at room temperature 2 to 3 hours without unwrapping. Other appetizers: Arrange on serving trays and thaw at room temperature about 1 hour.	Sandwich-type—2 to 4 weeks. Sausage, salami, smoked salmon, ham—3 to 4 weeks. Other types—2 to 4 months.
Biscuits Baked (unbaked not recommended, as will be smaller and less tender)	Make and bake as usual. Freeze before packaging.	To serve hot, heat unthawed biscuits in a 350°oven for 15 to 20 minutes.	2 to 3 months
Bread and Rolls Quick breads	Prepare as usual and bake to light brown: Gingerbread Nut and fruit breads Coffee cake Steamed breads Cool quickly. Wrap in moisture-vapor-resistant paper.	Thaw in wrapping at room temperature, or if wrapped in aluminum foil, heat in a 400° oven. Slice fruit and nut breads while partially frozen to prevent crumbling.	2 to 4 months
Muffins	Prepare as usual. Bake and cool. Package in moisture-vapor-resistant paper or container.	Thaw in wrapping at room temperature about 1 hour. Or heat in a 300° oven about 20 minutes.	6 to 12 months
Waffles	Bake to a light brown. Cool. Wrap individually or in pairs in moisture-vapor-resistant paper.	Heat without thawing in a pop-up toaster, under the broiler, or on a baking sheet in a 400°oven for 2 to 3 minutes.	1 to 2 months
Yeast breads and rolls, baked (unbaked yeast rolls not recommended; unless recipe is formulated for freezer storage	Prepare and bake as usual. Cool quickly. Freeze before wrapping.	Thaw in wrappings at room temperature, or, if wrapped in aluminum foil, heat in a 300° oven about 15 minutes for bread, 5 to 10 minutes for rolls.	6 to 8 months
Yeast breads, partially baked	Prepare as usual. Small rolls freeze best. Bake in a 275° oven for about 20 minutes. Cool quickly. Wrap and freeze.	Thaw in wrappings 10 to 15 minutes. Bake in a 425° oven 5 to 10 minutes or until lightly browned. If the undercrust of the rolls is too moist, bake on a cooling rack instead of a baking sheet.	6 to 8 months

Food	Preparation/Packaging	To Serve	Storage Time
Cakes Angel Chiffon Sponge	Make as usual. Cool. Do not use egg white in frosting. If frosted, freeze before wrapping. If unfrosted, wrap and freeze. If slices are frozen, place a double fold of moisture-resistant paper between slices. If tube pan has been used, fill hole in cake with crumpled moisture-resistant paper. Place whole cake in a box or carton to prevent crushing.	Thaw in wrappings on a rack at room temperature for 1 to 2 hours. Or, if not frosted and if wrapped in aluminum foil, thaw in a 300° oven 15 to 20 minutes. Frosted cakes may be thawed at room temperature or in the refrigerator. Remove wrapping if frosting begins to stick to it.	Egg white cakes— 6 months. Whole-egg cakes— 4 to 6 months. Egg-yolk cakes— 2 months.
Cheesecake	Prepare and bake as usual. Freeze before wrapping. Wrap and store in carton.	Remove wrap and thaw in refrigerator 4 to 6 hours, or ½ hour at room temperature. If stored in metal pan, dip bottom of pan in warm water to unmold.	4 months
Cupcakes, baked	Make as usual, but bake in paper cups for easier storage. Freeze before wrapping. Wrap individually or in pairs in moisture-vapor-resistant paper. Store in box that can be opened easily to remove just the number to be used.	Thaw at room temperature about 1 hour, or if not frosted and if wrapped in aluminum foil, heat in a 300° oven for 10 minutes.	2 to 3 months
Fruitcake, baked	Bake as usual. Freeze before wrapping; then wrap in moisture-vapor-resistant paper.	Thaw in wrapping at room temperature about 1 hour per pound of cake.	12 months
Shortened—including chocolate, nut and spice types, baked	Prepare and bake as usual. Cool. Do not use egg white in frosting. (Frosting and cake are best frozen separately. Thaw each and then frost the cake.) If frosted, freeze before wrapping. If unfrosted, wrap and freeze. If slices are frozen, place a double fold of moisture-resistant paper between the slices. Place whole cake in a box or carton to prevent crushing.	Thaw in wrappings at room temperature about 2 hours. Or, if not frosted and if wrapped in aluminum foil, thaw in wrappings in a 300° oven 10 to 15 minutes for layer cakes and 25 to 30 minutes for loaf cakes. Frosted cakes may be thawed at room temperature or in the refrigerator. Remove the wrapping if the frosting begins to stick to it.	2 to 4 months
Unbaked	Not recommended; when batter is frozen, volume of cake after baking will be smaller.		
Upside-down cake	Freezing not recommended.		
Cookies, Baked	Prepare as usual and cool. Package in cartons or plastic bags with moisture-resistant paper between layers and crumpled in spaces.	Thaw in wrapping 15 to 20 minutes if cookies are crisp type. They will be less crisp than cookies baked from frozen dough. Soft cookies may be placed on serving plate to thaw.	6 to 8 months
Unbaked (all types, except meringue)	For *refrigerator cookies,* form dough into roll. Slice if desired. Wrap and freeze.	Bake slices without thawing.	6 months
	For *drop* cookies, drop on baking sheet or prepare bulk dough. If cookies are formed, freeze on baking sheet. Store in moisture-vapor-resistant	Bake formed cookies without thawing in a 400° oven. Thaw bulk dough at room temperature until soft	6 months

(Continued on next page)

Food	Preparation/Packaging	To Serve	Storage Time
Cookies, Unbaked (continued)	carton with moisture-resistant paper between layers. Package bulk dough in rigid container or plastic bag.	enough to drop by spoonfuls on greased baking sheet.	
Creamed Dishes Meat, Fish, Poultry	Prepare as usual. Slightly undercook added food. If waxy rice flour is available, use it to replace half or more of the flour. Omit hard-cooked eggs and cooked potatoes. Cool rapidly by setting pan in cold running water or in ice water. Stir to hasten cooling, but don't beat in air. Pack in rigid, wide-mouthed containers. Cover with a single thickness of paper, cut to fit the surface. Leave head space. Lobster, crab, and shrimp will gradually toughen in storage.	Heat, from frozen or thawed state, in top of double boiler or in a 350° oven. If sauce has separated, stirring will make it smooth.	Chicken— 10 to 12 months. Shellfish— 1 to 2 months. Other— 4 to 6 months.
Custards	Not recommended for freezing since they may separate and curdle on thawing.		
Doughnuts	Raised doughnuts freeze best. Cake-type doughnuts may become slightly crumbly. Glazed doughnuts lose the glaze on freezing and thawing. Prepare all types as usual and cool. Package in plastic bags, or in rigid containers with crumpled moisture-resistant paper inserted in air spaces. If container is not of freezer material, wrap in moisture-vapor-resistant paper.	Thaw in a 400° oven, or in wrapping at room temperature. Roll glazed doughnuts in granulated sugar if desired.	3 to 4 weeks
Dressing (for meat or poultry)	Make as usual. Cool quickly by placing container in running cold water or in ice water. Package in moisture-vapor-resistant paper or in rigid containers.	Place in greased casserole before completely thawed. Add a small amount of water, cover, and heat in a 350° oven or heat in top of double boiler.	1 month
Fish Dishes Baked or boiled	Prepare as usual. Leave whole or in large pieces. Cool quickly by placing container of fish in running cold water or in ice water. Wrap in moisture-vapor-resistant paper, or package in plastic bags or rigid containers. If rigid containers are used, sauce or broth can be added. Be sure it covers the fish, and fill air spaces with crumpled moisture-resistant paper.	Unwrap and heat without thawing in a 400° oven 20 to 25 minutes.	1 to 2 months
Fish loaves	Prepare as usual. Do not put bacon strips on top. Pack in loaf pan; do not bake. Wrap in moisture-vapor-resistant paper, filling any air spaces with crumpled moisture-resistant paper, or place in plastic bags.	Thaw in wrapping in refrigerator for 1 to 2 hours. Unwrap and bake in a 450° oven for 15 minutes; then reduce heat to 350° to finish baking.	1 to 2 months
Flaked, in cheese or Creole sauce	Make as usual, keeping fat to a minimum. Slightly undercook vegetables. Cool quickly by placing container in running cold water or ice water. Use rigid wide-mouthed containers. Be sure fish is covered by sauce. Leave head space.	Partial thawing in package at room temperature will help to prevent over-cooking. Heat partially thawed or frozen food in top of double boiler or in a 400° oven about ½ hour.	4 to 6 months
Flaked, in cream sauce	See under Creamed Dishes above.		
Fried pieces or sticks	Fried fish may lose some fresh flavor and crispness during freezing; this is partly restored on reheating. Fry as usual, but do not completely cook. Cool quickly. Freeze on trays. Wrap pieces in moisture-vapor-resistant paper, or in plastic bags.	Place frozen sticks or pieces in a single layer in a well-greased baking pan. Bake in a 400° oven 20 to 25 minutes or until fish is heated through and crisp.	1 to 2 months

Food	Preparation/Packaging	To Serve	Storage Time
Frostings and Fillings	Do not freeze fillings containing cream or eggs. Frosting containing egg whites becomes spongy. Frozen frostings lose some gloss and ones with much granulated sugar may become grainy. Frostings containing confectioner's sugar freeze best. Cooked frostings may crack. Package in rigid containers or plastic bags.	Thaw in container in refrigerator.	1 to 2 months
Gravy	Since gravies tend to separate and curdle when thawed, it is better to freeze broth and make the gravy just before serving. If gravy is to be frozen, adding ¼ teaspoon gelatin to each quart of gravy reduces curdling. If waxy rice flour is available, use it to replace half or more of the flour. Fat separation occurs only when too much fat is used in relation to flour. Package in rigid containers.	Heat in top of double boiler. Break up the frozen blocks.	2 months
Macaroni or Spaghetti	Usually better to cook just before using. If they are to be frozen, undercook slightly. Freeze in cartons or plastic bags.	Thaw in sauce or in a steamer about 10 minutes.	1 month
Meat and Poultry Fried	Frozen fried meats and poultry may lose some fresh flavor and crispness. Fry as usual until almost done. Cool quickly. Freeze on trays. Wrap pieces in moisture-vapor-resistant paper or in plastic bags.	Thaw at room temperature. Place in a shallow pan and heat, without a cover, in a 350° oven for 30 to 45 minutes.	1 to 3 months
Roast	Roast as usual. Remove as much fat as possible. May be boned to save space, but keep pieces large. Turkey and other large fowl should be cut from the frame to save space. Ham and other cured meats often lose their color when frozen and become rancid more quickly than other meats. Gravy, sauce, or broth helps to keep meat from drying out and losing color. Dry (for short storage)—Package in moisture-vapor-resistant paper. With sauce or broth—Package in rigid containers. Cover sliced meat with sauce, gravy, or broth. Cover with a piece of crumpled moisture-resistant paper. Leave head space.	Thaw dry meat in wrapping in refrigerator or at room temperature. Or set container in water. If wrapped in aluminum foil, heat in a 325° oven. Thaw meat with sauce in refrigerator 5 to 6 hours or heat slowly on top of range or in oven.	2 to 4 months
Dressing, for meat and poultry	See directions on page 78 under Dressing.		
Combination meat dishes—stews, spaghetti sauce with meat or meatballs, ravioli	Make as usual, keeping fat to a minimum. Omit potatoes from stew. Slightly undercook other stew vegetables. Freeze meat balls and spaghetti sauce, and cook spaghetti just before serving. Cool rapidly by setting pan in running cold water or in ice water. Use rigid wide-mouthed containers. Be sure meat is covered with sauce or broth. Leave head space.	Partial thawing in package at room temperature will help to prevent over-cooking. Heat partially thawed or frozen food in top of double boiler or in a 400° oven.	4 to 6 months
Meat loaf	Make as usual. Bake or leave unbaked.	For unbaked frozen loaf, unwrap and put in pan. Bake in 350° oven for 1½ hours. To serve baked loaf cold, thaw in wrappings in refrigerator; to reheat, unwrap and place in pan unthawed in 350° oven for 1 hour.	3 to 4 months

Food	Preparation/Packaging	To Serve	Storage Time
Nuts	Shell. Package in rigid containers or plastic bags. Seal.	Thaw before using.	6 to 8 months
Pastry Unbaked	Make regular pastry or crumb crust as usual. Fit into pie pans. Prick pastry. Stack the pie pans with two pieces of moisture-resistant paper between each; then one crust may be removed at a time. Cover top pie crust with paper. Wrap stack with moisture-vapor-resistant paper. If preferred, several flat rounds of pastry may be stored on cardboard and separated with two pieces of moisture-resistant paper between each one.	Bake, still frozen, in a 475° oven until light brown. Or, fill and bake as usual. If frozen flat, set frozen pastry on pie pan until thawed and molded to pan.	6 to 8 weeks
Baked	Bake as usual and cool. Leave in pie pan or freeze before wrapping and remove from pan. Wrap in moisture-vapor-resistant paper, excluding as much air as possible. Storage in a box or carton will protect shells.	Thaw in wrapping at room temperature 10 to 20 minutes. Add filling.	2 to 3 months
Pies Chiffon	Make with gelatin base. Freeze before wrapping. Wrap in moisture-vapor-resistant paper or put in plastic bag. Store in carton.	Thaw unwrapped at room temperature for 1 hour.	2 weeks
Custard, Cream, and Meringue	Not recommended for home freezing.		

Fruit, Mince, and Nut	Make as usual, except that for very juicy fillings add an extra tablespoon of flour or tapioca or ½ tablespoon of cornstarch. This will help to prevent fillings from boiling over when pies are baked. Do not cut vents in top crust. Do not bake. Steam and cool light fruits before making pie.
	For *apple* pie: Dip raw apple slices
	   in mixture of ½ teaspoon ascorbic acid to
	   1 cup water. One cup will treat apples for
	   4 or 5 pies.
	For *peach* pie: Peel peaches without scalding. Slice. Mix with 1 tablespoon lemon juice or ¼ teaspoon ascorbic acid in 1 teaspoon water per pie.
	Freeze fruit pies in their pans. Wrap in moisture-vapor-resistant paper or put in plastic bag. Store in carton, or cover with second empty pan turned upside down and tape edges together.
		Cut vent holes in upper crust. Place on cooky sheet. Bake without thawing for 15 to 20 minutes in a 450° oven; then reduce heat to 375° and bake for 20 to 30 minutes more or until top crust is brown.	3 to 4 months (Mince, 6 to 8 months)

Pumpkin	Prepare pie shell and filling as usual. Have filling cold before adding it to unbaked pie shell. Package the same as fruit pies.	Bake without thawing, 10 minutes in a 400° oven; then reduce heat to 325° to finish baking.	4 to 5 weeks
Fruit pie fillings	Make as usual. Freeze in rigid containers. Leave head space.	Thaw just enough to spread in pie crust.	6 to 8 months
Pizza	Prepare as usual. Do not bake. Cool, if topping is warm. Wrap in moisture-vapor-resistant paper. Seal.	To bake, unwrap and bake unthawed in 450° oven for 15–20 minutes.	1 month
Potatoes Baked and stuffed	See under Guide to Freezing Vegetables on page 71.		

(Continued on next page)

Food	Preparation/Packaging	To Serve	Storage Time
Potatoes, (continued) French fries or shoestring	Cut strips rather small. Blanch or scald in boiling water for 1 to 2 minutes. Drain well. Fry quickly to light brown. Drain. Do not salt. Cool quickly. Pack in rigid container or plastic bag.	Spread on baking sheet. Heat unthawed and finish browning in a 475° oven for about 5 to 6 minutes, or brown in deep fat (watch carefully for spattering).	2 to 3 months
Mashed	Make as usual. Shape into patties or leave in bulk. Pack patties with 2 pieces of moisture-resistant paper between layers. Press bulk potatoes tightly into container in layers, with 2 pieces of moisture-resistant paper between layers. Press out air spaces. Place crumpled moisture-resistant paper on top.	Thaw just enough to slip into top of double boiler. Stir while heating. Or, fry patties slowly, without thawing.	2 weeks
New (very small)	See under Guide to Freezing Vegetables, page 71.		
Scalloped	Prepare and bake as usual until almost tender and a delicate brown color. Leave in baking dish. Cool quickly. Cover surface with moisture-resistant paper cut to fit. Wrap in moisture-vapor-resistant paper or put in plastic bag.	Place in cold oven, or partially thaw at room temperature. Add milk, if necessary. Complete baking.	2 weeks
Salads Fruit	Salads which freeze well are fruit salads which are served frozen with a base of cream or cottage cheese, whipped cream, mayonnaise, or gelatin combined with one of these (not a separate gelatin layer). Do not use apples, grapes, or nuts. Fit a piece of moisture-resistant paper over the top. Wrap in moisture-vapor-resistant paper.	Defrost in refrigerator about 1 hour, but serve before completely thawed.	6 to 8 weeks
Sandwiches, Closed For open-face sandwiches see "Appetizers"	Use day-old bread. Spread to edges with softened butter or margarine. Omit: crisp vegetables, hard-cooked egg white, tomato, jellies and jams. Mayonnaise tends to separate. Use a salad dressing. Wrap individually or in groups in moisture-vapor-resistant paper. Sandwiches may be carefully wrapped in double thicknesses of waxed paper if kept only a week or two. Keep them away from uneven moistness when thawed. Store in box or plastic bag.	Thaw at room temperature in wrappings 3 to 4 hours. Frozen sandwiches in a lunchbox will thaw in 3 to 4 hours and will help keep other food cool.	Cheese, ham, bologna— 3 to 4 weeks. Others— 3 to 6 months.
Sauces Dessert and meat	If flour is used in making sauce, see Gravy, on page 79. Since spices may change flavor over long storage, it is best to add them just before serving. Package in rigid container. Cover with crumpled moisture-resistant paper. Leave head space.	Thaw in package at room temperature, or heat in top of double boiler. Stir well if sauce tends to separate.	3 to 4 months
Soups and Purées	Omit potatoes. When possible, concentrate by using less liquid in preparing, or by evaporating liquid when cooking. Vegetables may be cooked and puréed for use in cream soup. Cool quickly by placing pan in cold running water or in ice water. Package in rigid containers. Leave head space. Or freeze in ice cube trays, and store cubes in plastic bag.	Heat without thawing; heat cream soups in top of a double boiler. If cream soup has separated, stirring will make it smooth. If concentrated, add hot liquid. Add potatoes or other vegetables needed. Vegetable purée may be thawed in covered casserole in a 400° oven or in double boiler; then add cream or milk.	4 to 6 months

Drying

Sun drying is probably the oldest method we know for preserving foods. When exposed to the sun and wind, fruits and vegetables just naturally shrivel and dry. And when most of the moisture is gone, spoilage is delayed (since removal of moisture actually inhibits microorganisms from growing) and the fruit may be stored.

Nature's simple process is essentially the way fruit drying is still done. Think of raisins coming from clusters of table grapes left out in the sun. For vegetables, oven drying is a more dependable method.

Sun drying still works for the ancient art of meat preservation, too. We call preserved meat "jerky." But we've included an easy version of jerky, using an oven instead of the sun.

Drying Fruit

Grapes, figs, and prunes dry nicely on their own when left exposed to sun and air. But fruits, like apples, pears, apricots, and peaches turn brown when exposed to air. This chemical reaction, called oxidation, also robs the fruit of flavor and vitamin C.

In order to dry these light fruits so they taste and look as good as dried fruits you can buy, you must halt the oxidation process. The most effective treatment known today is to expose the cut fruit to the fumes of burning sulfur. The sulfur prevents browning and also helps repel insects, speeds up drying time, and acts as a preservative. The drying process can be stopped while the fruit is still pliable, retaining most of its original shape, color, and vitamin C.

Sulfuring is the technique commercial fruit dryers use and is recommended for home fruit drying. If the technique is properly used, it is perfectly safe and leaves no harmful residue on the fruit. Directions for sulfuring fruits at home are given on the chart on page 86. The chart tells which fruits require it and the amount of sulfur to use.

The alternatives to sulfuring are all far less effective. Blanching fruit in steam before drying helps destroy the enzymes that promote oxidation; dipping fruit in antioxidants, like ascorbic acid (vitamin C), or salt helps retard darkening, but the fruits become soft and are hard to handle. If you want to try one of these alternatives, write for these publications:

Home Drying of Fruits and Vegetables (Extension Circular 332). Utah State University Extension Services, Logan, Utah 84321.

Home Drying of Fruits and Vegetables (E.M.

2313). Cooperative Extension Service, Washington State University, Pullman,Washington 99163.

The chart on page 86 gives you the information you'll need to produce delicious home-dried fruits. Some varieties give better results than others. Large-sized fruits need to be sliced or cut. Prunes have tough skins; before you dry them whole, they need to be dipped in a weak lye solution so tiny cracks form in the skin. (Directions follow; it's safe when done as directed.) Or you can halve the prunes and eliminate this step.

Select fully ripe but not mushy fruit—fruit that is in top condition for eating fresh. Underripe prunes, for instance, turn dark brown and puffy.

Sort and wash all fruit. Discard any that shows signs of spoilage unless it can be completely cut away.

For figs, grapes, and prunes

Line drying trays with a double layer of cheesecloth (available by the yard in fabric stores). The trays can be rimmed baking sheets, clean shallow cardboard or wooden boxes, or stackable trays made of fruit-packing lugs (see diagram on page 85). Spread fruit slightly apart on cheesecloth.

Lye bath for whole prunes. Combine 5 teaspoons lye (available in hardware stores) and 1 gallon water in a large stainless steel or enamelware kettle and heat to just below boiling. Wear rubber gloves to protect your hands, and be careful to avoid splattering. Place prunes in a wire strainer and immerse in the lye solution just until skins check or crack—about 5 to 15 seconds (if left too long, their skins will peel). Rinse *very thoroughly* under a strong stream of cold water and let drain. Spread on cheesecloth.

To dispose of lye solution, carefully pour it down a sink drain or toilet bowl. Rinse sink and utensils with large amounts of cold water.

Arrange trays in the sun, off the ground on benches or a picnic table if possible. To protect from insects, cover trays with a single layer of cheesecloth so cloth doesn't touch fruit. Check frequently; move trays when shaded.

If you live in an area where nights are relatively clear and nighttime temperature doesn't drop more than about 20° F below midday highs, you can leave trays outdoors or stack them and cover. If there's fog or the temperature is expected to drop more than 20° F, bring trays under cover.

If it rains, bring trays indoors, and if they need to remain indoors more than just briefly, cover with cheesecloth to protect from dust. The fruit will continue to dry—but much more slowly. Check frequently; if you see any mold forming, do this: mix 1 tablespoon sodium hypochlorite (available in drug stores) and 1 quart water.

Moisten a cloth with solution and wipe off mold. The solution will slow down (but not prevent) additional mold from forming.

The time it takes to dry fruit depends on its size and on the temperature and humidity. In hot areas, it may be done in two or three days; in cooler areas up to about seven days. Test for dryness, using guidelines in the chart on page 86. When dry, bring indoors and let fruit cool completely before packaging.

Store dried fruit sealed inside double plastic bags, in glass jars, or in plastic or ceramic containers (rinse containers in hottest tap water and dry well). Metal containers may be used if you package fruit in plastic bags first. Place a double layer of clear plastic film over mouth of a jar before putting on a metal lid.

Let fruit mellow for about two weeks before eating. Packaged fruit stored in a cool dry place, or refrigerator or freezer, should keep for about a year. Remember to check fruit often; discard any that turns moldy.

If the fruit is firmer than you like, "tenderize" it before eating by immersing in boiling water for about 15 seconds; then let dry on paper towels.

For apples, apricots, nectarines, peaches, and pears

Preventing oxidation by sulfuring (or an alternative method) is necessary before these fruits are put out to dry. Sulfuring requires that the fruit be arranged on wooden trays that, when stacked, allow fumes to circulate freely.

With a few alterations, wood fruit-packing lugs (about 17½ by 13½ inches) make excellent drying trays (see photograph on page 82). Check with your grocery store or build your own.

To prepare each tray, remove lug bottoms. From 1¼-inch-wide smooth pine lath, cut six pieces about 17½ inches long. Starting ½ inch from each side of the lug, nail lath about ⅞ inch apart across lug bottom. Use common (non-galvanized) nails to avoid corrosion caused by sulfur fumes. Cut four 1½-inch-long legs from 1-inch-diameter doweling and nail to bottom corners.

Each of these drying trays will hold about 1 to 1½ pounds whole apricots or about 15 to 18 pitted apricot halves. If you have a lug of apricots weighing 24 to 26 pounds and a sulfuring box with a capacity of eight trays, you'll need to do the job in three batches.

For sulfuring, you'll need a large cardboard box, such as the packing cartons large appliances come in—an oven or range carton covers five or six trays, and refrigerator or freezer cartons hold up to about ten trays (appliance stores are usually anxious to give cartons away). It should be free

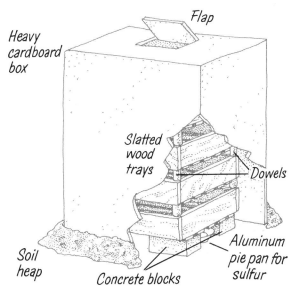

Heavy cardboard box

Flap

Slatted wood trays

Dowels

Soil heap

Concrete blocks

Aluminum pie pan for sulfur

of cracks or holes, but small ones can be covered with masking tape. Cut a flap in the box near the bottom so you will be able to reach inside to light the sulfur. Cut a flap the same size in top.

You'll need two concrete building blocks (about 8 by 8 by 16 inches), an 8-inch foil pie pan, and either pure powdered sulfur (available in hardware and some drug stores) or flowers of sulfur (from nurseries or garden supply centers); check label to see that it is at least 99.8 percent pure.

Sulfuring must always be done outdoors. Choose a place where there is unplanted dirt or gravel. Dig a shallow pit to hold foil pan. Place concrete blocks on either side of pit about 17

inches apart, then stack drying trays on blocks. Cover all with the cardboard box—it should be at least 1½ inches larger than the height, width, and length of the stack of trays.

After drying trays are made and your sulfuring box is prepared, you are ready to proceed. Line trays with a double layer of cheesecloth and arrange prepared fruit on cloth the same as for fruits that don't require sulfuring. The weight of cut fruit determines the total amount of sulfur needed (see chart on page 86). Put measured sulfur in the foil pan and place in prepared pit.

It is best to begin sulfuring in late afternoon or early evening so the fruit can remain in the box overnight after sulfuring. Stack trays of fruit on the blocks and cover with sulfuring box. Push dirt against bottom edges of box to seal. If box has bottom flaps, turn to outside and weight flaps with bricks to seal.

Open the two small flaps you cut in the box. Light sulfur with a match. After 5 minutes, peek through bottom flap to check that sulfur is burning; if not, relight. When the sulfur is burning well, close both flaps. Since the sulfur fumes can be highly irritating, keep children and pets away. The next morning, remove box and arrange trays in sun, following directions for untreated fruits.

Note: In areas where there is frequent rain, you may find oven drying your fruit a better method than sun drying. Since sulfured fruit cannot be oven dried, you will have to use one of the other ways to prevent browning as described in the publications listed on page 83. They also tell you how to dry fruit in an oven.

Dried Fruit Recipes

Harvest Pie

When fresh fruit is no longer in season for pie making, turn to those fruits you've dried.

1 can (16 oz.) unsweetened applesauce
1 cup chopped pitted dates
½ cup raisins and chopped dried figs
⅓ cup chopped pitted prunes
⅓ cup chopped dried apricots
¼ cup firmly packed brown sugar
2 tablespoons grated lemon peel
    Unbaked 9-inch pie shell
1 cup chopped pecans or walnuts
    Streusel Topping (recipe follows)

Combine in a saucepan the applesauce, dates, raisins, figs, prunes, apricots, sugar, and lemon peel; simmer uncovered over low heat for 15 minutes, stirring frequently. Cool. Pour fruit mixture into the unbaked pie shell. Sprinkle with chopped nuts and cover with Streusel Topping. Bake in a 375° oven for 30 minutes or until crust and streusel are browned. Makes about 8 servings.

Streusel Topping. Combine ⅓ cup firmly packed brown sugar and ½ cup all-purpose flour. Cut in 3 tablespoons butter or margarine with a pastry blender or two knives until particles are about the size of small peas. Squeeze small handfuls of the crumb mixture together firmly; then crumble evenly into coarse chunks over pie filling.

High-Energy Trail Logs

Backpackers will applaud these hearty little nuggets of energy. They can be served at home as snacks, too. Seal them in plastic wrap and store in the refrigerator for several weeks.

- ¼ cup dry-roasted cashews
- 1¼ cups walnuts
- 6 dried black figs
- ½ cup pitted dates
- ½ cup golden seedless raisins
- ¼ cup dried apples
- ½ teaspoon lemon juice
- 1 tablespoon dark or light rum
- 2 tablespoons powdered sugar or about ½ cup flaked coconut

Run nuts and fruit through the fine blade of a food chopper and mix thoroughly. Blend in lemon juice and rum. Using about a tablespoon at a time, roll the mixture into small logs, each about 2 by ¾ inch. Roll the logs in powdered sugar or coconut and allow to stand uncovered for one or two days to dry. Store in refrigerator or wrap tightly in foil or plastic film to carry on the trail. Makes about 2½ dozen.

Fruit-nut Sandwich

Spread filling on thin-sliced whole wheat bread layered with cream cheese. Serve open-faced, cut into strips. Tuck in lunch boxes or serve with coffee or tea.

In a saucepan, combine 1½ cups dried apricots, lightly packed, and 1 cup water. Simmer, covered, for 25 to 30 minutes, or until very soft and most of the water has evaporated—uncover if necessary for the last few minutes of cooking. Remove from heat, mash, and stir in ½ cup firmly packed brown sugar. Then stir in ½ cup chopped or sliced almonds. Makes about 1½ cups, enough for 8 sandwiches.

Drying Guide for Fruits

Fruit	Varieties Best for Drying	How to Prepare the Fruit	Treatment Before Drying	Test for Dryness
Apples	Firm varieties such as Gravenstein, Newtown Pippin, Winesap, Rome Beauty, and Jonathan	Peel, cut off both ends. Either cut out core and slice apples into ¼-inch-thick rings, or cut into ¼-inch-thick slices, removing core.	Sulfuring is preferred. Use 2 teaspoons sulfur for every pound of cut fruit.	Soft, leathery, pliable.
Apricots	Blenheim, Royal, and Tilton	Wash, cut in half, remove pits.	Sulfuring is preferred. Use 1 teaspoon per pound of cut fruit.	Soft, pliable—slightly moist in center when cut in half.
Figs	Adriatic, Calimyrna, Mission, and Kadota	Leave figs on tree; when fully ripe, and ready for drying, they fall to the ground. Wash, leave whole.	No treatment necessary.	Leathery outside but still pliable. Interior should be a little sticky but not wet.
Grapes	Thompson Seedless and Muscat	Wash, leave whole. Leave stems on until after fruit is dried.	No treatment necessary.	Raisinlike texture, wrinkled.
Nectarines and peaches	Freestone varieties	Wash, cut in half, remove pits. Not necessary to peel peaches but will result in better-looking dried fruit.	Sulfuring is preferred. Use 2 teaspoons sulfur for every pound of cut fruit.	Soft, pliable—slightly moist in center when cut in half.
Pears	Bartlett	Wash, peel, cut in half, remove core.	Sulfuring is preferred. Use 2½ teaspoons sulfur for every pound of cut fruit.	Soft, pliable—slightly moist in center when cut in half.
Prunes	French, Imperial, Sugar, Standard, Burton, and Robe de Sergeant	Halves: Wash, cut in half, remove pits. Whole: Check or crack skins in lye bath as directed on page 84.	No treatment necessary.	Halves: Flesh firm but still pliable. Whole: Flesh firm—pit will not slip when prune is squeezed.

Fruit Leathers

It's a cloudless morning with sunny weather promising to hold for several more days. You have a good supply of ripe fruit or perhaps some succulent but imperfect leftovers from canning or making preserves. It's an ideal opportunity to make fruit leathers.

This age-old process couldn't be simpler. The lightly sweetened purées of fruits and berries, spread in thin layers and left in the sun, dry into translucent sheets of fruit that are chewy and good.

Rolled sheets of these dried fruits, similar to our homemade ones, have been sold in some specialty food markets for several years and are now quite widely available. Here's how you can make your own fruit leathers.

Setting up

You need only a smooth level surface, such as a table; a place to put it in full sun; and a roll of clear plastic film. Tear off strips of the film, stretch it across the drying surface, and fasten with cellophane tape. To keep the fruit clean while drying, stretch a sheet of cheesecloth over it; you can secure it to two 2 by 4-inch boards on either side, taking care to keep it from touching the purée.

Preparing fruit

Wash fruit and prepare each as directed below; it should be fully ripe. Cut away any blemishes; then measure (up to 5 pints for any one batch). Add sugar and heat as directed for each fruit. Remove from heat and whirl (part at a time, if necessary) in a blender or put through a food mill or wire strainer; cool to lukewarm. Pour purée onto prepared surface and spread to ¼ inch thick (a full 5-pint batch covers a 30-inch-long strip of 12-inch-wide plastic film).

Apricots. Remove pits and measure halves; use 1½ tablespoons sugar for each cup fruit (1 cup sugar for 5 pints). Crush while heating to just below boiling (about 180° F).

Berries. Remove stems and measure whole berries; use 1 tablespoon sugar for each cup strawberries (½ cup sugar for 5 pints), 1½ tablespoons sugar for each cup raspberries (1 cup for 5 pints), or 2½ tablespoons sugar for each cup blackberries (1½ cups sugar for 5 pints). Bring strawberries just to full rolling boil. Boil other berries,

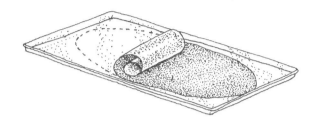

stirring, until liquid appears syrupy; then put through a food mill or wire strainer to remove some of the seeds; spread these berries about 3/16 inch thick.

Peaches and nectarines. Choose yellow freestone peaches, such as Rio Oso, Redhaven, Elberta; peel and slice to measure (do not peel nectarines). Use 1½ tablespoons sugar for each cup fruit (1 cup sugar for 5 pints). Crush while heating to just below boiling, about 180°F. (If liquid is thin, boil until it appears syrupy.)

Plums. Choose varieties with firm flesh, such as Santa Rosa, Mariposa, Nubiana; slice and measure. Use 2½ tablespoons sugar for each cup Santa Rosa (1½ cups sugar for 5 pints), about 1½ tablespoons sugar for each cup other plums (1 cup sugar for 5 pints). Crush while heating to just below boiling, about 180°F. (If liquid is thin, boil until it appears syrupy.)

The drying

It may take 20 to 24 hours to dry, depending on the fruit and the sun's heat. By the end of the first day it should be dry enough that you can loosen tape, slip a baking sheet underneath, and carry it inside; return to sun the next morning. When firm to touch, try peeling the fruit sheet off the plastic. It is sufficiently dry when the whole sheet can be pulled off the plastic with no purée adhering. (Don't leave in sun longer than needed.) In humid climates, you may need to finish the drying indoors. Set the sheets of fruit on pans in a 140° to 150° oven and leave oven door slightly open.

For storing. Roll up sheets of fruit leather, while on plastic film, then cover that with more plastic and seal tightly. Color and flavor keep well about one month at room temperature, four months in refrigerator, or one year if frozen.

Drying Vegetables

Drying vegetables involves different procedures from drying fruit and a little more work—you have to prepare, blanch, dry, package, and store vegetables. Like fruit, if vegetables aren't in prime condition for cooking, they won't be any good for drying. Although they can be sun dried, a better way of drying is to use a simple dehydrator—your oven.

If sun drying, you'll need temperatures of 100°F and relatively low humidity. If one or the other is unreliable, spoilage will probably occur before the vegetables can dry. It will take about three to four days for this process, and vegetables need to be chopped into small sizes no larger than ½-inch cubes. You must remember to bring the trays of vegetables into the house at night if the temperature outside drops 20° between day and night.

For *oven drying,* you'll need drying trays (directions to make them are on page 89), an accurate thermometer, and a small fan.

The charts on pages 90-91 will give you preparation steps required for each vegetable, as well as the best varieties to use, blanching methods and times, and tests to determine dryness.

First, you blanch

Blanching is the process of heating vegetables sufficiently to inactivate enzymes. If the enzymes are not inactivated, deterioration will result during drying and storage. Unblanched vegetables will have poorer flavor and color after they have been dried. Blanching may be done in hot water or in steam (directions follow). While water blanching usually results in more leaching of vegetable solids, it takes less time under kitchen conditions than steam blanching.

Directions for steam blanching

You'll need a kettle with a tight-fitting lid to use as a steaming container, and a colander, wire basket, or sieve that will fit into the steaming container.

Add 1½ to 2 inches water to the kettle and heat to boiling. Place the colander, loosely packed with vegetables, into the kettle and leave until they are heated through and wilted. Check the chart for blanching times. Test by cutting through the center of vegetable to see if it looks cooked (translucent) almost to the center.

Directions for water blanching

Use only enough water to cover the vegetables. Bring water to a boil and gradually stir in the vegetables, following directions on the chart for each vegetable. Reuse the same water for additional batches of the same vegetable when blanching, adding new water as necessary. Keep a lid on the container when blanching.

Step-by-step directions for oven drying

1) Load two to four oven-drying trays (see special feature, page 89) with 4 to 6 pounds of prepared

vegetables. Distribute vegetables evenly between the trays in a single layer. Don't dry more than one kind of vegetable at the same time unless drying times are the same (check chart on pages 90-91). Don't dry odorous vegetables (cauliflower or broccoli) with any other vegetable.

2) Place a thermometer on the top tray toward the back of the oven.

3) Preheat oven to 160° and add loaded trays. Prop open the oven door at least 4 inches.

4) Place a fan outside oven so air will circulate through the open door and across the oven. Change the fan's position from side to side and from top to bottom during the drying period.

5) Always keep the oven temperature at 140°. It takes less heat to keep this temperature toward the end of the drying period. (Watch temperature toward the end of period to prevent scorching.)

6) Check vegetables often and turn trays frequently to prevent scorching, especially at the end of period.

7) The time required for drying varies according to the type of vegetable, size of pieces, and load on the tray. The time at 140° varies from 6 to 16 hours.

Packaging vegetables

Remove vegetables from oven and pack as soon as they are cool. Use jars with well-fitting lids (canning jars). Coffee cans may be used if you package vegetables in plastic bags first. The dried vegetables should be packed into the container as tightly as possible without crushing. Then, to kill any possible insects (or their eggs), place the packaged dried vegetables in the freezer for 48 hours.

Storage of vegetables

Store containers in a dry, cool, dark place. If they are not stored in the dark, wrap all clear containers with paper or foil. Lower storage temperature extends the shelf life of the vegetables.

Carrots, onions, and cabbage deteriorate at more rapid rates than other vegetables and will generally have a shelf life of 6 months. Other vegetables will still be good after one year of storage. But as a general rule, plan on using the dried vegetables within 6 to 10 months.

If you are worried about storage space, remember that 1 pound of dried vegetables equals 8 to 12 pounds of fresh vegetables.

Nutritional changes in vegetables during drying

Neither the bulk nor energy-yielding properties of vegetables are affected by drying. Blanching will leach out some minerals and vitamins. To keep leaching to a minimum, blanch only as long as required. Try not to underblanch because the enzymes will not be inactivated and the vegetables will be inferior.

If you follow directions carefully, you will get a tasty, wholesome product.

Cooking dried vegetables

Dried vegetables are not as easily prepared as fresh, frozen, or canned ones. The removed water must be added back, either by soaking, cooking, or both.

Many vegetables may lose their fresh flavor during drying, so it may be an advantage to add seasonings during the cooking to enhance the flavor that does remain.

Root, stem, and seed vegetables should be soaked ½ to 2 hours in enough cold water to cover them. After soaking, simmer until tender, allowing excess water to evaporate. Greens, cabbage, and tomatoes don't need to soak. Just add enough water to keep them covered, simmering until tender.

How to Make Drying Trays for Oven Drying

Use wood, such as Douglas fir, that is clean, dry, and free from pitch and odors. Don't use resinous yellow pine.

The outside dimensions of the tray must be at least 1½ inches smaller than the inside width of your oven. When trays are loaded with vegetables and stacked in the oven, allow at least 2½ inches between trays and 3 inches of free space at the top and the bottom of the oven. The tray bottoms may be constructed of ¼-inch-wide wooden slats that are ½ inch apart (or made of stainless steel hardware cloth). Don't use galvanized screen, for the zinc coating may dissolve and contaminate the food.

To prevent sticking during drying, a "spray-on" vegetable oil may be used sparingly on the wood. Cheesecloth may be spread over the slats for drying smaller pieces of vegetables. Remember that drying shrinks the vegetable pieces, so they may fall between slats as they become dried.

Drying Guide for Vegetables

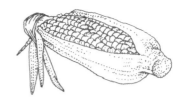

Vegetable	Varieties Best for Drying	How to Prepare and Treat	Test for Dryness (*Cool* before testing)
Artichoke, Globe	Only tender hearts are suitable	Cut hearts into ⅛-inch strips. *To blanch,* heat in boiling solution of ¾ cup water and 1 tablespoon lemon juice for 6–8 minutes depending on size.	Brittle
Asparagus	Only tender tips should be dried	Wash thoroughly and halve large tips. *To blanch,* steam 4–5 minutes. Water 3½–4½ minutes.	Leathery to brittle
Beans, Green	Use only tender stringless varieties	Wash thoroughly. Cut in short pieces or lengthwise. *To blanch,* steam 3½–4 minutes. Water 3 minutes.	Very dry, brittle
Beets	Use only small, tender beets	Cook as usual. Cool; peel. Cut into shoe-string strips ⅛ inch thick. Already cooked. No further blanching required.	Tough, leathery
Broccoli	Use young, fresh stalks	Trim and cut as for serving. Wash thoroughly. Quarter stalks lengthwise. *To blanch,* steam 5 minutes. Water 4½ minutes.	Brittle
Brussels Sprouts	Use small, tight, fresh sprouts	Cut in half, lengthwise through stem. *To blanch,* steam 6–7 minutes. Water 4½–5½ minutes.	Very dry to brittle
Cabbage	Copenhagen Market, Danish Ball Head, Golden Acre, Savoy Winningstradt	Remove outer leaves, quarter and core. Cut into strips ⅛ inch thick. *To blanch,* steam 2½–3 minutes or until wilted. Water 1½–2 minutes or until wilted.	Tough to brittle
Carrots	Danvers Half Long, Imperator, Morse, Bunching, Nantes, (Chantennary not recommended)	Use only crisp, tender carrots. Wash thoroughly. Cut off roots and tops; preferably peel, cut in slices or strips ⅛ inch thick. *To blanch,* steam 6–7 minutes. Water 5–6 minutes.	Tough, leathery
Cauliflower	Use small, fresh flowerettes	Prepare as for serving. *To blanch,* steam 4–5 minutes. Water 3–4 minutes.	Tough to brittle
Celery Both leaves and stalks may be dried	Use only crisp, tender stalks relatively free from "strings"; use small, green, leaves.	Trim stalks. Wash stalks and leaves thoroughly. Slice stalks. *To blanch,* steam 3–4 minutes. Water 2–3 minutes.	Brittle
Corn on the cob	Stowells Evergreen, Country Gentlemen, Golden Bantam. Ears should be young, tender and in milk stage.	Husk, trim. *To blanch,* steam until milk does not exude from kernel when cut, usually 5–6 minutes. Water 4–5 minutes.	Dry, brittle
Corn, cut	Use same varieties and prepare same as corn on the cob, except cut the corn from the cob after blanching.		
Eggplant		Wash, trim, cut into ¼-inch slices. *To blanch,* steam 4 minutes. Water 3 minutes.	Brittle

Vegetable	Varieties Best for Drying	How to Prepare and Treat	Test for Dryness (*Cool* before testing)
Horseradish		Wash; remove all small rootlets and stubs. Peel or scrape roots. Grate. No blanching needed.	Very dry and powdery
Mushrooms	Young, medium sized, freshly gathered. "Gills" pink, free of insects or any blackening.	Scrub thoroughly. Discard any tough, woody stalks. Cut tender stalks into short sections. Do not peel small mushrooms or "buttons." Peel large mushrooms and slice. *To blanch,* steam 3–4 minutes. Water 3 minutes.	Very dry and leathery
Okra		Wash, trim, and slice crosswise in ¼ to ⅛-inch strips. *To blanch,* steam 4–5 minutes. Water 3–4 minutes.	Tough to brittle
Onions	Creole varieties, Ebenezer, Southport Globes, Sweet Spanish, White Portugal (only onions with strong aroma and flavor should be dried)	Wash and remove outer "paper shells." Remove tops and root ends and slice ⅛– ¼ inch thick. No blanching needed.	Brittle
Parsley		Wash thoroughly. Separate clusters. Discard long or tough stems. No blanching needed.	Brittle, flakey
Peas	Use young, tender peas of a sweet variety (mature peas become tough and mealy)	Shell. *To blanch,* steam 3 minutes. Water 2 minutes.	Crisp, wrinkled
Peppers	*Red or Green:* California Wonder, Merimack Wonder, Oakview Wonder	Wash, stem, core. Remove "partitions". Cut into dices about ⅜ by ⅜ inch. No blanching needed.	Brittle
Potatoes	Russett Burbank, White Rose	Wash, peel. Cut into shoe-string strips ¼ inch in cross section, or cut in slices ⅛ inch thick. *To blanch,* steam 6–8 minutes. Water 5–6 minutes.	Brittle
Spinach and other greens (kale, chard, mustard)	Use only young, tender leaves	Trim, wash very thoroughly. *To blanch,* steam 2–3 minutes or until thoroughly wilted. Water 2 minutes.	Brittle
Squash, winter	Banana	Wash, peel, slice in strips about ¼ inch thick. *To blanch,* steam 3 minutes. Water 2 minutes.	Tough to brittle
	Hubbard	Cut or break into pieces. Remove seeds and seed cavity pulp. Cut into 1-inch-wide strips. Peel rind. Cut strips crosswise into pieces about ⅛ inch thick. *To blanch,* steam until tender.	Tough to brittle
Squash, summer	Crookneck, Pattypan, zucchini	Wash, trim, cut into ¼-inch slices. *To blanch,* steam 4 minutes. Water 3 minutes.	Brittle
Tomatoes, for stewing	Firm-ripe tomatoes with good color, no green spots	Steam or dip in boiling water to loosen skins. Chill in cold water. Peel. Cut into sections about ¾ inch wide, or slice. Cut small pear or plum tomatoes in half. *To blanch,* steam 2–3 minutes or until soft. Water 1–2 minutes or until soft.	Slightly leathery

Note: 8 to 12 pounds fresh vegetables will yield 1 pound dried.
Important: Cool the test piece before testing for dryness.

Making Jerky

To survive the grueling trek across the Sierra Nevada, Jedediah Smith and other "mountain men" often relied on leathery morsels of sun-dried meat they had carefully stored in their saddlebags days before.

Beef jerky is still a staple in the packs of today's mountain men—backpackers, skiers, and campers—and a popular snack for armchair sportsters, too.

In the modern version of this ancient method of preserving meat, your oven dries the thin, seasoned, strips instead of the sun.

You can also dry fully cooked ham (see separate directions). Because you start with smoked meat, ham jerky requires no additional seasoning from a marinade. Serve it as a snack to nibblers or crumble it to flavor or garnish other dishes as you would bits of bacon. (If the ham is quite salty, eating the ham jerky on a hike may make you thirsty.)

Partially freezing the meat before cutting makes it easier to slice evenly. Cut with the grain of the meat if you like a chewy jerky; cut across the grain for a more tender, brittle product.

This recipe makes the quantity of meat you can dry in one oven.

Oven-Dried Jerky

The following recipe is for lean cuts of beef (flank, brisket, or round steak), venison, and the white meat of turkey or chicken.

1½ to 2 pounds lean, boneless meat (see above), partially frozen
¼ cup soy sauce
1 tablespoon Worcestershire
¼ teaspoon each pepper and garlic powder
½ teaspoon onion powder
1 teaspoon hickory smoke-flavored salt

Trim and discard all fat from meat (it becomes rancid quickly). Cut the meat in ⅛ to ¼-inch-thick slices (with or across the grain, as you wish). If necessary, cut large slices to make strips about 1½ inches wide and as long as possible.

In a bowl, combine the soy sauce, Worcestershire, pepper, garlic powder, onion powder, and smoke-flavored salt. Stir until seasonings are dissolved. Add meat strips and mix to thoroughly coat all surfaces. (Meat will absorb most of the liquid.) Let stand 1 hour or cover and refrigerate overnight.

Shaking off any excess liquid, arrange strips of meat close together but not overlapping, directly on the oven racks or on cake racks set in shallow, rimmed baking pans.

Dry meat at the lowest possible oven temperature (150° to 200°) until it has turned brown, feels hard, and is dry to the touch (about 5 hours for chicken and turkey, 4 to 7 hours for beef and venison). Pat off any beads of oil. Let cool, then remove from racks and store airtight in plastic bags or in a jar with a tight-fitting lid.

Keep at cool room temperature or in the refrigerator until ready to use; it keeps indefinitely. Makes about ½ pound.

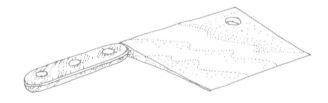

Oven-Dried Ham Jerky

Ask your butcher to slice 1½ to 2 pounds fully cooked, boneless ham ⅛ to ¼ inch thick. (Or you can slice leftover ham.) Trim and discard all fat. Cut the slices into strips about 1½ inches wide and as long as possible. Lay ham strips close together, but not overlapping, directly on the oven racks or on cake racks set in shallow, rimmed baking pans. Dry ham at the lowest possible oven temperature (150° to 200°) until it feels hard and snaps readily (5 to 5½ hours). Pat off any beads of oil. Let cool; then remove from racks and store airtight in plastic bags or in a jar with a tight-fitting lid.

Keep at cool room temperature or in the refrigerator until ready to use; it keeps indefinitely. Makes about ½ pound.

Sun-Dried Jerky

This jerky "cooks" in the sun all afternoon and comes out quite spicy because of all the goodies in the marinade. For those living under cloudy skies, there are directions for oven drying at the end of the recipe.

1 pound very lean top round steak
4 teaspoons salt
1 teaspoon pepper
1 teaspoon chile powder
1 teaspoon garlic powder
1 teaspoon onion powder
¼ teaspoon cayenne
3 dashes liquid smoke
½ cup water

Trim the meat carefully, removing any fat or connective tissue, and place in the freezer to partially freeze (about 1 hour). While the meat is in the freezer, mix the salt, pepper, chile powder, garlic powder, onion powder, cayenne, and liquid smoke in a bowl. Pour in water, stirring to blend well.

When the meat has firmed enough to make thin slicing easy, cut across the grain in slanting slices about ⅛ inch thick. Place the strips in the marinade, stir, cover, and chill several hours or overnight, stirring occasionally.

Remove strips from marinade, drain, and spread on cake racks placed on baking sheets. Expose to hot sun until thoroughly dry but still somewhat pliable (6 to 7 hours). Arrange cheesecloth over the strips while they are drying to protect from insects, and either cover strips or bring them inside at night.

For oven drying, arrange meat on racks the same way you would for sun drying above and place in a 150° to 200° oven with the door slightly ajar. Dry until a test piece cracks but does not break in two when you bend it (about 6 hours). Let cool, remove from racks, and store airtight at room temperature or in the refrigerator. Makes about 8 ounces of jerky.

Drying Fresh Herbs

If you have an abundance of fresh herbs on hand in summer, you may want to preserve some for later use.

Drying is the easiest method of preserving herbs. You simply expose the leaves, flowers, or seeds to warm, dry air until the moisture is gone. The best time to harvest most herbs for drying is when the flowers first open. Ones having long stems—such as marjoram, sage, savory, mint, and rosemary—can be dried in bunches. Cut long branches and rinse in cool water, discarding any leaves that are dead or have lost their color. Tie the ends of the stems together into small bunches and hang them upside down in a warm, dry room where they won't be exposed to direct sunlight. A warm, even temperature is best. Air should circulate freely around the drying herbs to absorb their moisture without destroying their oils, so don't hang them against a wall. If you dry herbs outside, bring them inside at night so the dew won't dampen them. To avoid collecting dust on the drying herbs, place each bunch inside a paper bag, gathering the top and tying the stem ends so that the herb leaves hang freely inside the bag. Cut out the bottom of the bag or punch air holes in the sides for ventilation.

After a week or two, the herbs should be cracking dry. Carefully remove the leaves without breaking them; then store in sealed containers.

Tray drying is best for seeds, such large-leaved herbs as basil, and short-tipped stems that are difficult to tie together for hanging. You can either remove the leaves from their stems or leave them attached, but spread only one layer of leaves on each tray. If you attempt to dry too many at once, air will not reach them evenly, and they will take longer to cure. Screens or trays can be made to any size, using window screening or cheesecloth for the drying deck.

Every few days, stir or turn the leaves gently to assure even, thorough drying. It should take a week or so for them to dry completely, depending on the temperature and humidity. When leaves are crisp and thoroughly dry, take off racks.

Seeds can be spread on the trays or screens in a thin layer and dried in the same way as leaves. When dried, carefully rub seed capsules through your hands, blowing away chaff.

Microwave ovens are a new and faster way to dry herbs. Rinse the herbs as for bunch or tray drying, shaking off excess moisture. Put no more than 4 or 5 herb branches in the oven between two paper towels. Turn on oven for 2 to 3 minutes; remove from oven and place herbs on a rack. If not brittle and dry when removed from oven, repeat microwave drying 30 seconds more. Then store as for regular dried herbs.

Index

A Handy Metric Conversion Table

To change	To	Multiply By
ounces (oz.)	grams (g)	28
pounds (lbs.)	kilograms (kg)	0.45
teaspoons	milliliters (ml)	5
tablespoons	milliliters (ml)	15
fluid ounces (fl. oz.)	milliliters (ml)	30
cups	liters (l)	0.24
pints (pt.)	liters (l)	0.47
quarts (qt.)	liters (l)	0.95
gallons (gal.)	liters (l)	3.8
Fahrenheit temperature (°F)	*Celsius temperature (°C)*	*5/9 after subtracting 32*